WRITING ON YOUR FEET

Reflective Practices in City as Text™

A Tribute to the Career of Bernice Braid

WRITING ON YOUR FEET

Reflective Practices in City as Text™

Edited by **Ada Long**

Series Editor | Jeffrey A. Portnoy
Georgia Perimeter College

**National Collegiate Honors Council
Monograph Series**

Manufactured in the United States

National Collegiate Honors Council
100 Neihardt Residence Center
University of Nebraska-Lincoln
540 N. 16th Street
Lincoln, NE 68588-0627
www.ncnchonors.org

Production Editors | Cliff Jefferson and Mitch Pruitt
Wake Up Graphics LLC

Cover and Text Design | 47 Journals LLC

Cover Photos by Roy Borghouts Fotografie
from the Master Class Innovators 010 Conference,
Rotterdam University of Applied Sciences–Netherlands

International Standard Book Number
978-0-9773623-6-3

TABLE OF CONTENTS

INTRODUCTION

Ada Long

City as Text™ (CAT) is one of the earliest structural forms of experiential learning created and practiced in the United States. Developed within the context of the National Collegiate Honors Council and modeled on the writings of Paulo Freire, Clifford Geertz, and David A. Kolb, CAT was the brainchild of Bernice Braid in the mid-1970s. In the intervening decades, CAT has energized more than thirty conferences, twenty-nine Faculty Institutes, and thirty-three Honors Semesters just within the NCHC. Campuses and organizations across the country have also had the wisdom to borrow or steal this form of experiential education in countless adaptations. Two previous NCHC monographs have described the methods and practices of CAT or CAT-based experiential education: *Place as Text: Approaches to Active Learning* (2000 and 2010) and *Shatter the Glassy Stare: Implementing Experiential Learning in Higher Education* (2008). This monograph explores the centrality of writing in the process of active learning.

City as Text experiences at the NCHC conferences are the most condensed form of Bernice Braid's unique brand of active learning. Before each conference, she collects relevant background readings that do not tell people what to expect on a site but give them some information and questions with which to get started. She then arranges a panel at the conference to provide orientation for the hundreds of CAT participants, an orientation that includes descriptions of the four major strategies of her unique brand of discovery: Mapping, Observing, Listening, and Reflecting. Participants then fan out into the city in groups of three or four to visit sites for which Braid has provided basic information about transportation, possible expenses, and sometimes local people available for interviews. The small groups then return to the conference hotel for some writing (mostly note-taking in this context), then a debriefing in a larger group, and finally a meeting of the whole group of participants, where representatives from each site report their findings and insights.

This basic structure is expanded in the five-day format of Faculty Institutes, designed to show teachers and administrators how to practice CAT principles and strategies on their home campuses. The Faculty Institutes include several site explorations and group debriefings along with three written assignments (First Impressions, Observations, and Turning Point essays). Recursive writing is key to the success of Faculty Institutes, pushing faculty to consider not only what they see in the field but the lenses through which they see it. Like all CAT experiences, the Faculty Institutes are not just about place but also about self and about the dynamic relationship between place and self, a relationship that requires private examination in the act of writing and then public expression in sharing the writing with the whole group. Each Faculty Institute culminates in a collection of Turning Point essays that is distributed to all participants.

The Honors Semesters are far more ambitious, requiring a sixteen-hour curriculum that includes a City as Text component, twelve hours of modular coursework, and an independent-study thread that culminates in a major research project. As in the Faculty Institutes, the focus on recursive writing is essential; participants come back again and again to analyze, recalibrate, and transform initial impressions as awareness of place, self, and the relationship between them deepens and expands. In an Honors Semester, students write several papers focusing on their first impressions—papers that are more ambitious and developed versions of the kind of note-taking that conference attendants produce during their CAT experiences—as well as two or three Turning Point essays and then a culminating paper reflecting on all their previous writing. The major research project for the semester is also often tied to their earlier reflective pieces and, unlike typical term papers, emerges from weeks of extensive explorations, recursive writing, peer-collaboration, intensive reading, and consultation with relevant experts.

This monograph focuses primarily on the Faculty Institutes and Honors Semesters that foster CAT experiences, but all manifestations of this pedagogical strategy share basic elements: focus on a broad theme, background reading, explorations, experts as supplements to personal experience, reflections on experience through group discussions, ambitious writing projects, collaboration, and interdisciplinarity. All CAT-centered educational experiences also feature four primary strategies in a set of instructions that is distributed at conferences and institutes:

1. **Mapping**—You will want to shape a mental construction, during and after your explorations, of the primary kinds of buildings, points of interest, centers of activity, and transportation routes (by foot or vehicle); sketching your own map might be helpful in this construction. You will want to look for patterns of building use (housing, offices, shops, parks, recreation, etc.), traffic flow, and social activity that may not be apparent on any traditional map. Where do people go, why do they go there, and how do they get there?

2. **Observing**—You will want to look carefully for the unexpected as well as the expected, for the familiar as well as the new. You will want to notice details of architecture, landscaping, social gathering, clothing, possessions, decoration, signage, and advertising. Try to answer the following questions: Does everybody seem to belong? Do some people seem lost or out of place? Why? Who talks to whom? In what ways is social interaction encouraged or discouraged? What feeling do you get about people as you watch them? Are they stressed, purposeful, interesting, lonely? Try to identify why you get these feelings about people.

3. **Listening**—You will want to talk to as many people as you can and to find out from them what matters to them in their daily lives, what they need, what they enjoy, what bothers them, what they appreciate. Strike up conversations everywhere you go. Imagine yourself as somebody looking for a job or a place to live (try to find a local newspaper), and ask

about such matters as where to find a place to live, where to find a cheap meal (or an expensive one), what the politics of the neighborhood are (do people like their neighborhood organization? the mayor? do they like working or living here?), what the history of the neighborhood is, what the general population of the neighborhood is like (age, race, class, profession, etc.), what people do to have a good time. An important strategy is eavesdropping: How are people talking to each other? What language(s) are they using? What are they talking about? How are they connecting to (or disconnecting from) their surroundings as they converse?

4. **Reflecting**—Throughout your explorations, keep in mind that the people you meet, the buildings in which they live and work, the forms of their recreation, their modes of transportation—everything that they are and do—are important components of the city environment. They are part of an ecological niche. You want to discover their particular roles in this ecology: how they use it, contribute to it, damage it, and change it. You want to discover not only how but why they do what they do, what they see, and how they see it. Like all good researchers, make sure that you are conscious of your own biases, the lenses through which you are seeing and judging, and that you investigate them as thoroughly as you investigate the culture you are studying.

Reflecting—the final and necessary step of the CAT experience—is the primary focus of this monograph.

Reflection takes place in several stages: (1) individual analysis and synthesis of observations and insights; (2) discussions and debriefings with fellow participants; and (3) written texts. In Faculty Institutes and Honors Semesters, the texts are recursive, moving from First Impressions to Observations and then to Turning Point essays. In addition, participants share their writings at each stage so that public presentation and interchange connect the writing to the collaborative explorations. The writing makes sense of the experience in a way that individual reflection and group discussions cannot; it is both the key step and the culmination of the experiential process. The writing also gives the experience its accountability and integrity. When participants become authors, they reveal themselves; they move beyond personal experience and commit themselves publicly to a point of view, to the process of observation and analysis that led to the point of view, and to the cultural and intellectual framework within which the process occurred.

Bernice Braid, the creator and presiding genius of City as Text, describes the architecture and architects of this kind of reflective writing in her chapter "History and Theory of Recursive Writing in Experiential Education." While providing the background, theory, purpose, and value of recursive writing in the context of CAT, she conveys the spirit of an educational strategy that has captured the imaginations of thousands of students and teachers since 1976. The essential concept—that teachers can and should abandon the glorious project of telling other people how much they know—is deceptively simple. Braid explains the precise dynamics of setting up a learning experience and then relinquishing control to the students so that they learn how to teach themselves, so that their voices are the ones that matter. She lays the intellectual and practical groundwork for all of the following chapters just as she laid the groundwork almost forty years ago for the unique brand of experiential education known as City as Text.

John Major follows with a chapter called "Claiming a Voice through Writing," in which he reflects on his experiences and on the essential role of writing in the 1984 United Nations Semester subtitled "From Urban to Global Community." Major offers a candid and personal narrative about his first days in the Honors Semester and his awakening sense of himself, his community, and his world. All of the students involved in this kind of experiential learning, Major says, are outside their power circle, removed from their history, background, and established identity. Everybody is vulnerable, everybody has to create a new identity, and reflective writing is the path to this new identity. He places this kind of writing within the intellectual framework—generated by Hannah Arendt, Christopher Hitchens, and others—of discourse on creative tensions between private and public, insider and outsider, native and immigrant. At the same time, he provides a moving account of John Major—the shy boy from a small Ohio town—in Brooklyn, New York, September of 1984, as he started to get his personal, intellectual, and civic bearings by exposing himself in writing. This particular form of imagining/writing empowered him and others to find a voice, to know it was heard, to know it mattered, to fit it into a community, to become a member of a democracy, to belong to a culture.

The chapter on "The Role of Background Readings and Experts" provides discussion of the unconventional use of outside resources in the City as Text framework. As in any academic setting, reading assignments include scholarly texts, but, at least at the outset, the readings are truly "background" in nature, addressing issues peripheral or aslant to the subject at hand and not providing right answers or pre-interpretations. Similarly, students engage in dialogue with experts after they have explored and discovered on their own; ideally, experts respond to the observations and analyses that students have formulated in the field.

The success of City as Text—given its unorthodox approach to writing, background reading, and expert opinion—depends entirely on faculty members who are trained, willing, and able, in the words of Sara E. Quay, "to make changes to the very nature of their craft." The training takes place in faculty development workshops called NCHC Faculty Institutes, which Quay describes as "'short courses' on CAT." In her chapter "The Beginner's Mind: Recursive Writing in NCHC Faculty Institutes," Quay describes the difficult task for teachers of returning to a state of not-knowing, of becoming a peer and participant along with students. Writing assignments that reflect and mimic the texts that students produce cast faculty members back into the role of learners, not only creating empathy for their students but also showing them the excitement and effectiveness of learning when authorities are not doing the learning for them. Quay describes the Faculty Institutes, including her first one, and analyzes the three-part recursive writing that creates the dynamic transformation from lecturer to learner in a Faculty Institute.

While Quay describes the practice of recursive writing in Faculty Institutes, Ann Raia describes this practice in the longer and more ambitious context of Honors Semesters in her chapter "Assigning, Analyzing, and Assessing Recursive Writing in Honors Semesters." In the sixteen-week, intensive, and interdisciplinary context of an Honors Semester, the basic principle of moving from impressions and observations to the analytical and self-aware writing that occurs in Turning Point essays follows the same dynamic as in Faculty Institutes but involves multiple iterations of this process within a longer-term, tightly knit community of students and faculty. A key difference is also that the students must earn grades and that the grades must have academic legitimacy while at the same time accounting for the kind of personal, social, and cultural evolution that takes place in an Honors Semester. Raia provides examples of assignments, thoughts about assessment, and a case study of one student's progress through recursive writing assignments toward deeper readings of himself, his peers, and New York City.

Demonstrating the innovative and unconventional ways that writing can be incorporated into an Honors Semester, Robyn S. Martin's chapter, "Finding Appropriate Assignments: Mapping an Honors Semester," describes the cultural mapping assignment in Writing the Canyon, one of the course options for students in the Grand Canyon Honors Semester. Students created colored maps of "geological, geographical, and cultural resources that they deemed important to their semester's experience"; they then wrote about the significance of the choices they had made in producing their maps and discussed each other's maps, questioning and explaining the choices that each student had made and why. Based on these maps and on their close observations throughout the semester, the students produced cultural artifacts that included poems, found objects, paintings, photographs, and songs, once again writing about what choices they had made and why as well as sharing their artifacts in a final public presentation. The process of recursive writing was thus melded in a real way with the mapping process that is fundamental to City as Text.

In the following chapter, "Adapting City as Text™ and Adopting Reflective Writing in Switzerland," Michaela Ruppert Smith gives an example of mapping and reflective writing on another continent and at another level of education: an International Baccalaureate school in Geneva. Smith and her colleagues used the CAT format to shape a student exploration of three sites in Zurich, including a restaurant called "Blindekuh," where the wait staff is blind and the customers dine in total darkness. This experience renders a dramatic example of mapping as "a metaphor for a personal voyage of discovery, of learning how to stand on foreign ground and find a new touchstone, a new perspective from which to see." Smith describes and illustrates the process of mapping and the crucial role that writing plays in solidifying the new sense of self that such mapping engenders in students.

The chapter "Writing as Transformation" contains insights into the impact of reflective writing within the City as Text experience through narratives by former students in four different New York Honors Semesters between 1981 and 2003. Echoing John Major's chapter "Claiming a Voice through Writing," the first two describe the process of self-definition that emerges from writing about and sharing site-based explorations. Rebekah Stone, in "1984 United Nations Honors Semester," leads off with the story of her arrival in New York City from Columbia, South Carolina, and the stages of liberation, self-doubt, and confidence that grew out of her finding a new voice through writing, a voice that eventually she could use to understand and accept the background she had been so eager to escape. In "2003 New York Honors Semester," Nicholas Magilton describes his progressive awareness of writing as a means to discover both place and self as he moved from a small town in Iowa to Iowa State University to Rome and then to the Honors Semester in New York, where he now lives and works as a landscape artist, using the observational skills he learned in writing assignments and field explorations.

The last two essays in "Writing as Transformation" provide a perspective different from the first two. In "1981 United Nation

Honors Semester," Nancy Nethery describes her arrival in New York from the University of Georgia and the different roles she tried on as "writer, club girl, art lover, human rights advocate, scholar," roles that flourished as she adapted to city life, isolated her when she returned to Georgia, and continue to define her more than thirty years later. Given her numerous selves, she chose to practice writing not as an act of self-expression but as a scholarly exercise, and she provides a moving illustration that writing as self-revelation can feel and be dangerous. Finally, in "2001 New York Honors Semester," Brittney Pietrzak from the University of Alabama at Birmingham, who arrived in New York one week before 9/11, recounts the effects of that trauma on her experience of the semester. In the vivid and terrifying aftermath at Ground Zero, she found stability and comfort only in her camera, which became her means of expression, providing her a new and permanent perspective on the world that other students achieved through writing.

The chapter by Gladys Palma de Schrynemakers—"Experiential Learning, Reflective Writing, and Civic Dialogue: Keeping Democracy on its Feet"—looks toward the future and the usefulness of City as Text in preparing people to adapt to a rapidly changing and expanding world. She argues that the traditional academic lecture formats, with teachers as pontificators and students as receptacles of wisdom, are inappropriate to the needs of the global and technological culture in which teachers need to be preparing students and themselves for the responsibilities of deliberation, democracy, and civic responsibility. City as Text, she suggests, is forward-looking in its focus on independent and collaborative learning, achieved through direct observation, continuous dialogue, and recursive writing. CAT requires that we all "begin again" and that we "put aside our old assumptions and look at ourselves and our world with new eyes" so that we can "redefine our civic opportunities and responsibilities."

"The Whole Journey" offers three sets of the kinds of writing— First Impressions, Observations, and Turning Point essays—that are the primary subject of this monograph. These writings—by Sara

E. Quay, Ada Long, and Joy Ochs—focus on Faculty Institute experiences in Las Vegas/Death Valley, Nevada; Iquitos/Madre Selva, Peru; and Miami/the Everglades, Florida.

One final note: As indicated in the title of this monograph and in the first reference of each chapter, the National Collegiate Honors Council has trademarked City as Text™ in an attempt, as CAT has grown more popular nationally and now internationally, to indicate its integrity as a particular pedagogy developed and practiced within the NCHC and to rein in an unfortunate temptation to give this name to simple tours or to assignments that send students out into a city without necessary structure, purpose, reflection, discussion, and writing. As we hope this monograph illustrates, City as Text is a site-based form of experiential education that requires rigorous training of its facilitators and practitioners.

REFERENCES

Braid, Bernice and Ada Long, eds. *Place as Text: Approaches to Active Learning.* Lincoln: National Collegiate Honors Council, 2010. NCHC Monograph Series. Print.

Freire, Paulo. *Pedagogy of the Oppressed.* Trans. Myra Bergman Ramos. New York: Herder and Herder, 1970. Print.

Geertz, Clifford. *The Interpretation of Cultures: Selected Essays.* New York: Basic Books, 1973. Print.

Kolb, David A. *Experiential Learning: Experience as the Source of Learning and Development.* Englewood Cliffs, NJ: Prentice-Hall, 1984. Print.

Machonis, Peter, ed. *Shatter the Glassy Stare: Implementing Experiential Leaning in Higher Education.* Lincoln: National Collegiate Honors Council, 2008. NCHC Monograph Series. Print.

WRITING ON YOUR FEET

Reflective Practices in City as Text™

CHAPTER 1

History and Theory of Recursive Writing in Experiential Education

Bernice Braid

City as Text™ (CAT) was born in a time when higher education was rethinking its modes of operation. In the 1970s a new relationship between teachers and learners emerged in discourse about knowledge and discovery that examined critically the culture of the academy. In the larger cultural context leading up to celebrations of the country's Bicentennial, American educators interrogated classrooms, disciplines, and pedagogical practices in light of a growing awareness of cultural change. The spirit of the 60s opened up a sense that active alternatives to passive learning could be mechanisms for significantly expanding the nature and scope of learning.

Paulo Freire's arguments contrasting "liberating" and "banking" educational practices resonated with this shift in sensibilities about student-faculty interactions: "The more students work at storing the deposits entrusted to them, the less they develop the critical consciousness which would result from their intervention in the world as transformers of that world" (60). Freire's sense was that students' creative impulse, their capacity to develop perspective, and their inclination to see themselves as agents of change were all hampered by the "banking" approach of the professoriate. These insights, articulated as the country was finalizing events and projects meant to express the reach of its bicentennial identity, percolated widely in academic circles as educators embarked on an activist revision of modes of inquiry.

Freire argued that students "may perceive through their relations with reality that reality is a process, undergoing constant transformation" (61). The implications of this argument had a major influence on a small group of faculty members in the National Collegiate Honors Council (NCHC) who were designing and implementing the first National Honors Semester: the fall 1976 Washington Bicentennial Semester (WBS). The group composed a set of strategies for grasping the scope of this Bicentennial celebration:

- Students had to move out into the world to take note of it.

- What they saw/collected in the field had to be juxtaposed with what they were learning through readings and lectures in the classroom.

- How they thought about their experiential and academic sources of information had to be recorded as part of their own learning process.

- Their written record had to become part of the group's larger discussion in sessions focused on the theme of the whole Semester, which was selected because it was profoundly central to that site.

- These discussions had to bring together into the same discourse the students' observations about all the disciplines represented, about their living situation, and about their own active investigations.

- What they were seeing, thinking, and feeling in the nation's capital had to be seen as refracted through the lens of what they brought with them from their home territory along with preconceptions about the nation and American culture.

Simply put, in order to consider the theme critically, students had to investigate in multiple and active ways: challenging authority, collecting and analyzing unmediated information, supporting their findings with evidence, and integrating these findings into a larger context. The issue of lens—who is looking at what and how—had to be a conscious dimension of the discourse. The complex structure of NCHC Honors Semesters emerged as a vehicle for integrating diverse disciplinary learning focused on a shared site-specific theme and explored as thoroughly in the site as in the seminars. The structure emphasized writing that aimed to record observations and details in context; to interpret, analyze, and substantiate these details; and to uncover the observers' perspectives on both what they were viewing and their own way of seeing.

Much has been published about the Honors Semesters. Colleagues have launched versions of their own, locally and internationally. The key integrative instrument, which by 1978 was called City as Text, has been adapted widely, at least in principle, and its use has proliferated in events ranging from conferences to campus orientations. This monograph focuses on one specific dimension of the entire CAT enterprise: the importance of reflective writing that is instrumental in the transformative process. The framework of an Honors Semester, as amplified here, reveals structural elements that undergird the power of reflective writing when it is an articulated part of an analytical process dealing with on-site, problem-based learning.

Typically the theme addressed by courses, readings, and CAT fieldwork has grown out of a specific site. The nation's capital in the year of America's Bicentennial, for instance, was arguably the ideal location for students to follow and analyze cultural issues of race, power, cultural promotion, and the process of change in both law and custom. From studying with a constitutional lawyer to recording local children's recess games in an inner-city elementary school, from thinking about the impact of the Civil Rights Movement to living in a city still rife with poverty and violence, students were in a crucible of cultural change in the year 1976. They came from all over the country to Washington, D.C., most of them visiting the area for the first time. Their residence off campus, yet in the District of Columbia, offered a three-dimensional laboratory in which they eventually recognized themselves as participants or agents in the process of change.

As facilitators, the professors emphasized and enacted the importance of recursivenes in repeated visits to local schools, in discussions, and in writing assignments about what students noted over time. Seminars became frameworks within which student voices bounced off one another. Small teams inevitably revealed divergent perceptions. Disparities between concepts about Americana and life on Washington's streets led to debate that sparked return visits to institutions and neighborhoods. Students' writing reflected the value of primary research in shaping a profile of the nation's Bicentennial as it unfolded. Theoretical and scholarly readings about how people live and what they produce necessarily contrasted with the raw reality of what students observed and experienced in the streets where people worked, lived, and played. The teachers in this scenario were leaders but also participants in an emerging understanding of "place," an understanding heavily informed by the students' deepening sense of who lives how and where. Faculty shared their adventure with students, eventually seeing themselves as facilitators in a new light: as co-participants and co-investigators.

Lessons learned from this initial experiment were adapted and formalized in a single course that promoted integrative learning—City as Text—and, within that course, the "writing on your feet" component on which this monograph focuses. Field-tested in 1978 and thenceforth a formal seminar plus field laboratory in all Honors Semesters, CAT is the locus of the recursive exploration/writing/discussion sequence that drives field observation and primary research. Students spend much time mapping: neighborhoods, folkways, local economics, local organizational structures, politics, and education. These inquiries, which include impressions during a walkabout, readings of respected theorists and researchers, and interviews of local residents, frame and contextualize the students' findings about the unifying theme in all their courses and provide a foundation for topics students select for semester-long research projects.

For instructors, preparing to teach the integrative seminar is freighted. Not only are they conceptualizing course readings on a theme examined in situ from divergent disciplinary viewpoints, but they are devising intersections with partnering courses and designing independent explorations that engage students in the field and that can amount to at least a third of the overall instructional program. The experiential dimension is part of the architecture of all the courses but is central to the CAT course, which is the integrative seminar.

The facilitator of the CAT course is an especially present absence since the goal of discovery is implemented by repetitive reflective written exercises that emphasize the lens of the writer. The students, more than the facilitator, establish the flow of discovery. Students share their differing accounts of a single incident, thus providing the basis of class discussions; they pay considerable attention to variations among their accounts and to contradictory interpretations that suggest disquieting multiple truths about viewpoint, human interactions, and social fabric. This disaggregation of what had initially seemed to be a single shared experience is unsettling, especially among a group heavily dependent on one another and living together as strangers in unfamiliar territory. It provokes students to return to the site, rethink their way of seeing, and begin to think about process, lens, and point of view. The power of writing begins with the recordkeeping but strengthens exponentially as part of the framework of comparing, rethinking, and self-consciously examining experiences undertaken in the public arena of the seminar.

Writing on their feet begins as a relatively simple exercise in recording: what is seen, who is there with the observers, who the observers are, how they function, how what is seen is interpreted, and what in the already recorded details supports the writers' interpretation. A brief question appended to instructions for this writing

7

directs attention to whether the authors have been in such a situation before, how they reacted then, how they might react differently the next time this sort of event might occur, and why. Written records become the texts in seminar discussions as students examine multiple viewings of the same scene, note anomalies and concurrences, and explore resultant issues of viewpoint in some depth.

The facilitator's role here becomes that of *agent provocateur*: one who prods the reporter, pushes the comparisons, and asks outsider questions without providing or even having an answer to questions raised by the texts under discussion. Why people choose to go through an educational process that involves reflective writing is inconsequential; what happens to people once involved is surprising, unpredictable, in some ways uncontrollable, and that is why it works. The control belongs to the student, not the teacher/architect who sets the structure and creates the context.

Students are intrigued by this mapping/reflecting/re-mapping once they overcome some initial panic: an exercise that is not graded is terrifying for honors students, and observations are normally not graded although more formal analytical papers are. Students gain confidence as they get caught up in the excitement of the questions they can answer after several mappings of the same place: How do people in this neighborhood earn a living? What services are readily available to them? Where do they mingle? What do they do there? Do they seem to feel safe? Are they comfortable, wary, or aloof? What makes you think so? Students discover their talents as chroniclers, and initial insecurity yields to a sense of triumph.

Understanding is a process in which preliminary impressions, questions, reconsideration, interpretation, and analysis are essential. CAT is like a laboratory experiment whose goal is the comprehension of unfamiliar phenomena: details are recorded in the time and place where they are seen, but they are not meaningful unless they form patterns. The patterns in turn must be examined carefully, tested for evidence that substantiates them, questioned, and reexamined before they become fixed. New questions lead to revisiting old sites and to new observations that may or may not validate preliminary impressions.

8

Unlike controlled experiments and much more like ethnographic studies, the context itself is uncontrollable; it might well need to be presumed, assessed, reconsidered, and deciphered before generating any assertion about it. What reflective writing adds to the sequence is that it places a premium on the explorer's capacity to measure the personal frame of reference as a contributing factor: the viewer's level of anxiety, for instance, and stereotypes about the actors in an event based on clothes or accents or tones of voice. The sense of self-in-the-scene is a significant contributory factor to impressions and interpretations. Being a stranger in a strange land, which the explorer always is, influences both the context and content of the interaction recorded, producing distorted eyewitness accounts. Unless the explorer recognizes this influence, the experiment yields suspect information.

Ultimately, just as instructors have anticipated, the walkers in a walkabout come to see that understanding is a process. Being in the world means being conscious of the world, as Freire argues: "'Problem-posing' education, responding to the essence of consciousness—*intentionality*—rejects communiqués and embodies communication." It epitomizes the "special characteristic of consciousness: being *conscious of* . . . consciousness as consciousness *of* consciousness" (66–67). An active approach to learning in Freire's model "involves a constant unveiling of reality" and leads to "*critical intervention* in reality" (68).

At this moment of consciousness, students know themselves to be participant-observers and are perhaps uncomfortable with this knowledge as it takes shape in debriefings and discussions of reflective writing assignments. Their sense of being instrumental in spite of themselves, when they acknowledge that their presence, smile, scowl, or camera played a part in the unfolding scene of which they were a part, transforms them. After roughly a half-dozen such discussions, they think of themselves as involved, as actors with definable roles, and as interested rather than disinterested observers. Often the very neighborhoods where they have returned for multiple observations become the subjects or settings of final projects in one or more courses.

In Freire's terms, "Problem-posing education bases itself on creativity and stimulates true reflection and action upon reality, thereby responding to the vocation of [people] as beings who are authentic only when engaged in inquiry and creative transformation. . . . [P]roblem-posing theory and practice take [people's] historicity as their starting point" (71). The power of probing any city, place, or region yields transformative results when students engage with place directly, see themselves as investigators, and reflect on their role in creating their sense not just of the place but of themselves as they interact with it. As students participate in this process, they change the way that they know places. In one of his most persuasive statements, Parker J. Palmer asserts: "I do not believe that epistemology is a bloodless abstraction; the way we know has powerful implications for the way we live. I argue that every epistemology tends to become an ethic and that every way of knowing tends to become a way of living" (25).

In an Honors Semester, faculty members ask students to explore, map, interpret, and analyze the world they inhabit and to repeat this assignment until this world feels like their own. Over time, a transformation in how students know and live occurs and is traceable in their reflective writings. The final assignment of the integrative seminar in which students review all their writing chronologically invariably reveals this transformation.

The title of this monograph refers to the existential dynamic of experiential education caught in moments like snapshots. When students capture not only what they see but how they see it by asking themselves what accounts for their observations, they turn their cameras on themselves. The several attempts to freeze their own thinking, when reviewed at term's end, reveal both to them and to their cohort the ambiguities of engagement with the world. The process is penetrating, leaving them with a residue of insight into their own way of being in the world. That insight strengthens their confidence and bolsters their sense of themselves as discoverers.

In the writing sequence for CAT, the pivotal role of Turning Point essays is their power to furnish instrumentality to explorers engaged in making sense of the radically new, unfiltered information that field experiences plunge them into. Recording their own evolution over time, identifying which specific event was a catalyst for what they see as a change in their ways of knowing, and discussing in seminar some examples that the entire group has identified is, in Clifford Geertz's phrase, "eye-opening":

> To see ourselves as others see us can be eye-opening. To see others as sharing a nature with ourselves is the merest decency. But it is from the far more difficult achievement of seeing ourselves amongst others, as a local example of the forms human life has locally taken, a case among cases, a world among worlds, that the largeness of mind, without which objectivity is self-congratulation and tolerance is a sham, comes. (16)

The power of raw experience, caught and conveyed in writing almost simultaneous with an experience, is that authenticity becomes a standard of judgment. Students must invent a vocabulary to express what they have observed, felt, and now see about situated knowledge. They also have a record available for review and comparison as they engage further with a new environment. The recursiveness of the exercise has an impact on consciousness because the chain of experiences recorded reveals nuanced shifts in viewpoint occurring through time.

Students come away from an Honors Semester with a sense of themselves as agents of change. Alumni are emboldened as well as grateful for the opportunity to have discovered in themselves a capacity to connect with the world and to have experienced the excitement of discovery itself.

REFERENCES

Freire, Paulo. *Pedagogy of the Oppressed.* New York: Continuum, 1985. Print.

Geertz, Clifford. *Local Knowledge.* New York: Basic Books, 1983. Print.

Palmer, Parker J. "Community, Conflict, and Ways of Knowing." *Change Magazine* Sept./Oct. 1987: 22–27. Print.

CHAPTER 2

Claiming a Voice through Writing

JOHN MAJOR

I still remember the moment as if it were yesterday: I sat mid-row, somewhere among the thirty-seven other students, within the banked seating of an auditorium at Long Island University. It was a Wednesday, September 5, 1984. I was a naive and gangly twenty-two-year-old student, an international studies major from a small town in southern Ohio who had never left the country, much less lived in New York. Now, suddenly, I found myself in downtown Brooklyn, across the street from the hubbub of the Fulton Mall, a pedestrianized shopping district, as diverse a world as any I could conjure. The previous evening, many of us had ventured a further ten-minute walk. Through rows of tony Brooklyn Heights brownstones lay the Promenade, a ribbon of footpath suspended over the Brooklyn-Queens Expressway that offered vast, open-skied vistas of the high-rises of Manhattan, the Statue of Liberty, the Brooklyn Bridge. Standing there, taking it all in as the sun slipped past the horizon and dusk descended to blanket the city, I felt a surge of having gotten to the place where I had long dreamed I wanted to be.

If it were a movie, a swell of orchestral music would have followed, complete with a lingering, poignant close-up and a fade to black.

The next morning, Bernice Braid, director of LIU's Honors Program, the host of our Semester ("The United Nations Semester: From Urban to Global Community"), called us to order. She asked us to go around the room and introduce ourselves, to say a sentence or two about who we were. The night before, we had played a similar game at a mixer in the dorm. Sitting in clusters scattered on the floor of the Resident Director's room, we were asked to introduce ourselves to each other: Where were we from? What were we studying? What was our favorite band? Our favorite soup? Somehow I managed to get through this exercise. Although I was quiet and reserved amid the chaos and cacophony, I spoke to three or four others and started feeling more comfortable, as if I might fit in. They were smart, interesting, funny—from Iowa, Kansas, and Illinois, studying political science, education, urban planning—maybe not so different from me.

But this introduction was different. This time the spotlight would be shining on me in front of everyone, if only for a brief minute or two, and in that brief time I needed to define myself. Immediately, I scanned the room and counted—how long did I have to script my speech? I felt flush, a bit dizzy, even panicked, and my mind raced to find some words.

I have no memory at all of what I said that day. Something short and straightforward, I'm guessing. I didn't have it in me to be witty or profound under pressure. No doubt it was all I could do to muster the volume to state my name.

Although this moment is a blur of sense memory as imprecise and hazy as an impressionist's canvas, I do remember what I wrote about the incident several weeks later. The class was City as Text™, the overarching seminar taught by Braid, and the assignment was to write about a "critical incident" from some time during the program orientation. "Identify a turning point," we were instructed. "Write about it in detail, asking yourself not only what happened but also how the incident made you feel. What beliefs did it challenge? Did the experience reinforce your prior beliefs or make you see things differently?"

Any number of experiences might have qualified as "critical" by this definition: an NGO briefing on nuclear disarmament; guided visits of New York City synagogues, churches, and mosques; panel discussions at the U.N. that demonstrated the intractability of Mideast conflict; a small group "treasure hunt" for Henry Moore sculptures that happened to be on display in public parks throughout the five boroughs. The one I settled on was that opening session. It was hard to know how personal I could be. I decided to go for broke. I wrote about what it feels like to be someplace new, the fear that comes from being parachuted into a group of people without knowing exactly how you fit in. I wrote about my frustration with finding a way to sum up who I was. Part of this annoyance derived from the inadequacy of words and my feelings of clumsiness in summoning them, but I also wrote about frustration with myself. I was a quiet introvert when I arrived for the U.N. Semester that September, and I had resolved to use this time as an opportunity for change. Now, here I was, barely two weeks in, and already I sensed that I was floundering. I wrote about how this moment on Day One left me with questions about the nature of change.

A few days later, we gathered for our City as Text course. Braid read aloud one of the critical incident essays, scrubbed of the author's identity, that she wanted us to discuss. The essay was mine. The next half-hour was spent in lively classroom discussion, the other students using my text as the basis for describing their own experiences. It probably won't come as a surprise when I report that many of them felt the same as I did.

What is the point of this story? Why do I still remember this episode almost three decades later? One reason is the sense of empowerment I felt in that moment. Yes, there was immense pride in having my words shared with this group I so desperately wanted to fit in among. But the real sense of empowerment I felt had to do with taking a moment of utter insecurity and alienation and finding, through writing and storytelling to this group, a way to sense that I belonged. Hearing others deploy my words as a point of departure for discussing their own feelings gave me a voice I did not know I had.

This experience was at odds with my education up to that point. More often than not, the practices I had been assimilating were predicated on a formulation of knowledge under conditions of detachment and objectivity, a belief that knowledge was impartial, like an Archimedean ideal. The preference was for a point of view outside oneself, what the late political theorist Iris Marion Young characterized as "a point of view outside concrete situations of action, a transcendental 'view from nowhere' that carries the perspective, attitudes, character, and interests of no particular subject or set of subjects" (100). This kind of thinking values abstraction. The ideal is a theory capable of dissolving the world into the general, the universal, the transcendent.

The depersonalization of ideas and opinions often extends even into our ordinary lives, affecting, for example, the kind of political conversation we might have with friends and neighbors. Journalist Christopher Hitchens recounted in an article for *Harper's*:

> At a dinner party, one is seldom told—and one is never to ask—how and especially why I just voted in the last primary or national election. Instead, one spends the evening at a certain clever, cool remove from the stuff of democratic politics—swapping back and forth across the table numbers gleaned from the CNN or ABC or Times Mirror poll. (45)

We do not speak in our own voice; our public opinions become more like predictions than deliberations. We begin to take more delight in reporting what we perceive to be the beliefs of others than revealing what we ourselves might believe. That missing voice, which I believe is the real stuff of democratic politics, is what the CAT form of writing offered me and my fellow students. Instead of treating stories as irrelevant or as verbiage to be waded through, this writing is premised on the notion that the stories themselves are artifacts through which students engage in civic conversation. The stories are the medium through which they claim their voice.

At the same time, however, this experience offered me an insight into the value of listening to my peers. How did they experience certain moments we shared in common? Did their observations jibe with mine? What conclusions did they draw from their experiences? Did these conclusions challenge my own ways of thinking? I remember another incident, a month into the semester, that will illustrate the point. Encouraged by our teachers to explore the city, a few of us decided to venture into Brownsville, a neighborhood in the heart of Brooklyn where a listing told us there was going to be a street fair. When we got there, the "street fair" turned out to be nothing more than a block party set among the high-rise housing projects. Our presence was conspicuous, and, after the group got separated, rightly or wrongly some of us judged the situation unsafe and headed back to LIU. Later, others returned and reported having heard shots fired. They were understandably shaken, felt abandoned by those who left early without them, and voiced their distress back at the dorm. Presented with another assignment in our City as Text course, I found this Friday night outing an opportunity to work through the multiple interpretations of this incident and to think about the basis for each. It was also an opportunity to integrate some of the concepts from our other coursework. In this case, I felt that the ideas we were discussing about the social contract provided a framework for considering what had happened and why some people might have read the text of this incident in particular ways.

Writing with such questions as a guide is a strong antidote to the comfortable retreat into abstraction. Too often that tendency signals intellectual closure, the abstract being premised on a broad inclusiveness that stifles alternative considerations and effectively eliminates variation. Our City as Text critical incidents emphasized particularity. Examining issues from the standpoint of others involves paying close attention to the subtle features that differentiate the perspectives. This approach is a gentle, inductive one, examining the limitations and contingencies of the particular as a way of bridging and building from the self to the group. Listening to others' stories and using them as reference points in navigating one's own thinking is neither a "view from nowhere" nor a "view from anywhere." Rather, the shared narratives become opportunities to view ourselves from the very places that others in our community inhabit.

17

Part of this process is to undertake a form of conscious "homelessness" in which observers/writers place themselves intentionally in the role of the immigrant. Typically, the immigrant is rendered in the simplest terms: either "outsider" or "assimilated," alien or a member, one of them or one of us. What I am proposing here is a more nuanced understanding that grows out of the work of Hannah Arendt and is a condition characterized by disorientation, discomfort, and estrangement. To be "homeless" in this way is to observe from a privileged position within the city walls but then question from the stance of an outsider who, though unfamiliar with customs and practices, is determined to make sense of them.

Ultimately, "homelessness" also creates the opportunity for self-reflection by immigrants scrambling to assess what their new circumstances mean to their sense of identity. Homelessness produces discomfort and bears an emotional cost. "Among these costs," Manfred Stanley writes, "is a certain primordial loss of innocence: the innocence of thinking that life is always going to continue in the manner to which one is adapted, the innocence of assuming that people's actions are always controlled by their intentions, the innocence of assuming one's identity and sense of worth can be taken for granted" (251). This loss of innocence is not some trivial side effect that we regret and wish we could eliminate; instead, it is the feature that both animates the immigration experience and provides the essential link to participation in a community. The loss of innocence provides a moment in which critical understanding is possible; to lose one's innocence is to encounter something new, something different, something which does not fit into the comfortable notions of how things work that we have constructed for ourselves over time.

In these moments, we experience several feelings at once. One is a sense of estrangement: where are we (figuratively and literally), and why are things no longer as we expected? Another is a sense of wonder and discovery: exactly how are things different now and what accounts for this sudden turn of events? What happens in these moments, then, presents an opportunity for asking questions where no questions presented themselves before. What once seemed natural now must be re-examined, and what once seemed commonsense might now need to be reconfigured. Of course, this process may also lead to other feelings: perhaps a sense of loss, of having to reevaluate and relinquish cherished modes of thought or comfortable patterns of behavior; a sense of frustration at having placed oneself in the midst of such unknowns; a sense of pride at having successfully negotiated this new environment and the unexpected features within its terrain; or a sense of hope for what is to come.

We attempt to give expression to these moments through what Stanley labels "crystallization": narratives of the sort that City as Text writing encourages (250). An exchange with others is critical; it clarifies that, despite crossing between worlds and feeling a sense of homelessness in unfamiliar terrain, we are not permanently alone, nor for that matter are we fully submerged into some amorphous mass that dissociates us from who we were. Our stories act like a form of currency, the unit of exchange through which we capture the drama and emotions of our experience, attempt to invest it with meaning, and offer it to others.

Moreover, as we engage in these exchanges, we erect a set of shared experiences that, in time, transform our set of individual selves into a public body. I do not mean that we are just a community. I also mean that, out of this collective experience and knowledge, our practices are transformed as well. I am thinking, for example, of "public" as it appears in the writing of David Matthews, president of the Kettering Foundation, where "the public is not simply a thing; it is a capacity" (122). Matthews makes this point through a pair of conceptual distinctions. First, he observes that the public is the antithesis of the private, recalling that the latter term's basis lies in concepts meaning "personal" and "secret" (122). Second, Matthews notes that the classical root of "public" is *pubes*, a term implying maturity and thus "the ability to understand the consequences of individual actions of others, the ability to see beyond ourselves" (122).

"Public" and "private," then, are not so much polar opposites as corollaries, elements of a unified whole in which individual, personal considerations are recognized but do not preclude considerations of others' values and beliefs, which are equally valuable. Because we know the fellow members of our community at some depth, the "others" that we are considering are not some nebulous, undefined assembly. They are our neighbors, maybe even our friends. Part of the Honors Semester experience involves a communal living arrangement, and contentious issues often arose at our town meetings. As the semester progressed, members of the group occasionally reminded us that, even if we all agreed about a certain issue in a particular discussion group, a specific missing classmate might very well disagree, and so we would posit how we might take that person's viewpoint into account. Arendt describes this imagining of a contrary voice as having "the imagination to go visiting" (43), which is a process of taking the time to consider the viewpoints of others standing where I am not, viewpoints known to us because of our collective history. Without opportunities to share our experiences and to communicate bits of ourselves through crystallizing narratives, our CAT group conversations would have lacked a certain depth and nuance, and our decisions would have lacked an element of consensus that gave them force.

Thirty years ago, I sat down and tried to tell a story. It was a chance to convey my complicated feelings, and my words resonated with others who heard them, giving them the opportunity to share their stories and convey complicated feelings of their own. The collection of such moments over those fifteen weeks in Brooklyn is why so many of us who participated in that Honors Semester still remain in touch after all these years. Those assignments represented a different model of what education could be. They were an invitation to join a larger conversation. They were a signal that we each had a voice that deserved to be heard.

REFERENCES

Arendt, Hannah. *Lectures on Kant's Political Philosophy*. Ed. Richard Beiner. Chicago: U of Chicago P, 1989. Print.

Disch, Lisa Jane. *Hannah Arendt and the Limits of Philosophy.* Ithaca: Cornell UP, 1994. Print.

Hitchens, Christopher. "Voting in the Passive Voice." *Harper's* (April 1992): 45–52.

Matthews, David. "The Public in Practice and Theory." Spec. issue of *Public Administration Review* 44 (1984): 120–25. Print.

Stanley, Manfred. "The Rhetoric of the Commons: Forum Discourse in Politics and Society." *The Rhetorical Turn: Invention and Persuasion in the Conduct of Inquiry.* Ed. Herbert W. Simons. Chicago: U of Chicago P, 1990: 238–57. Print.

Young, Iris Marion. *Justice and the Politics of Difference.* Princeton: Princeton UP, 1990. Print.

CHAPTER 3

The Role of Background Readings and Experts

ADA LONG

SOME GENERAL IDEAS

Reading in the service of active learning and reflective writing is roughly the opposite of the reading habits that most of us develop as tourists. When we are planning to visit new places as tourists, we typically read books to find out what there is to see, and then we go there to see it. Generations of tourists, including Mark Twain and Bertrand Russell, have seen the world with Baedekers tucked under their arms. Henry James once wrote, when arriving in Switzerland at the Hotel Byron, that he had "Baedeker in hand, to 'do' the place" (70). Later generations would arrive with Arthur Frommer's *Europe on 5 Dollars a Day* to find places to stay, eat, and sightsee. Although tourists who use such guidebooks have been satirized as mindless gawkers in, for instance, James's fiction or in Doug Mack's *Europe on 5 Wrong Turns a Day*, most of us want a place to start and a guiding idea for our travels, a framework within which to interpret all that will be new and challenging to us.

We count on experts in the same way we count on travel guides: to tell us what to see and do, to identify what is important in the places we are about to visit, and to explain why it is important, what it means. We take classes, attend lectures, do Google searches, ask friends, and watch documentaries to gear up for travel experiences.

This kind of pre-travel expertise is typically absent and discouraged in active-learning experiences, and the kinds of readings assigned are perhaps perverse in withholding the reassurances of guidebooks. Reading assignments follow the direction suggested by Emily Dickinson:

> Tell all the Truth but tell it slant—
> Success in Circuit lies
> Too bright for our infirm Delight
> The Truth's superb surprise
> As Lightening to the Children eased
> With explanation kind
> The Truth must dazzle gradually
> Or every man be blind—
> (#1129, 855–56)

Readings address the places to be discovered without providing a map, guidebook, recipe, or formula for understanding it. They tell a little bit of the story, tantalizing the readers simultaneously to discover and create the bigger pictures that gradually emerge in the course of discussions and especially in recursive writing.

The absence of authoritative texts or experts before learners set about discovering on their own is of a piece with the absence of authorities generally in that process of discovery. Just as the hardest lesson for facilitators to *get*, unless they have first experienced this kind of learning, is the role of staying on the sidelines, so the absence of defining texts is an unnerving deprivation for those of us trained in academia. We want to bestow wisdom, insight, and truth to the uninformed; giving such gifts is our reason for living—or at

24

least for being college teachers. Without it, we feel vulnerable and useless . . . until we have tried seeing what it is like to listen rather than talk. The experience of trusting others to come to insights and wisdom and truths on their own is exhilarating; the pleasure comes from creating contexts in which this can happen rather than articulating or imposing our own views, and it comes not from giving lectures but from hearing and reading the always surprising and interesting views of others.

A common objection when teachers experience their first introduction to active learning is that it is not academically serious, that it marginalizes hard research and scholarship in favor of squishy touch-and-feel stuff. On the contrary, the research and scholarship are at least as hard as in traditional education; they simply occur at a different point of the process. Instead of front-loading the students' heads with authoritative texts and expert opinions, the students first find out what they can discover on their own, after which they have personal incentives to read the texts and hear the experts. The teachers need to be more rigorous, more knowledgeable than in a standard classroom because they have to provide not only the readings they can plan beforehand but new ones that arise from unexpected directions and from student demands for more information. In other words, rather than prepackaging course material to play to one's own strengths, the active teacher has to know as much as possible in order to serve as a constant consultant to curious students with a wide variety of interests.

Active learning thus makes unfamiliar demands on teachers. Careful planning and research are crucial to structuring the learning experience, but, rather than seeking out the standard authorities on a subject, which is a comparatively easy undertaking, the active teacher looks for texts that hint and tease, texts that do not give students answers but instead get them started in asking the right questions. A similar challenge is scheduling experts who will help students think rather than think for them and deciding when, during the learning experience, these experts can be most helpful. Finding experts who can listen as well as talk, who can take seriously the opinions and insights of newcomers to their field of interest, is a chore. Fortunately, if it turns out that an expert is a bully after all, no harm is done; since students encounter experts only after they have experienced and reflected on their own, they have typically developed enough confidence to avoid being intimidated. The students already have some faith in their own expertise.

The learner-as-expert approach does not attribute knowledge to students who do not have it; instead, it attributes to them the seriousness of purpose that we associate with expertise. As scholars, we never read one book and decide that it is the truth; we read another, and another, and we compare and analyze and evaluate and struggle with inconsistencies as we move toward a perspective that is ours and that we care about. This process is what makes us experts, and it is a process our students can practice just as we do. We need simply trust them to practice it.

PRACTICAL MATTERS

Selecting the readings for an active-learning experience is one of the most creative and demanding roles of the teacher. Having decided on a site and a focus for the project, the planner gets to read widely and eccentrically, consult with colleagues and experts, and come up with a list of relevant and interesting texts. The next step is culling the list, and a good place to start weeding is the authoritative texts, the ones that explain all there is to know about a place. The teacher needs to have read such texts, and the students may well read them as the course proceeds, but they do not belong as introductory materials. Ideally the readings represent a variety of genres and open questions more than provide answers.

In instances where the students are faculty members—as is the case, for instance, in NCHC Faculty Institutes—readings include texts describing methodologies of active learning. These might include *Place as Text: Approaches to Active Learning* (edited by Braid and Long) or David A. Kolb's *Experiential Learning: Experience as the Source of Learning and Development* or *Shatter the Glassy Stare: Implementing Experiential Learning in Higher Education* (edited by Peter A. Machonis). What faculty members take away from an active-learning project includes skills in putting together such an experience for their own students; having read something about this approach to learning before doing it is helpful even though, in almost all cases, it does not make much sense to them until they have done it themselves and can then reexamine the readings with greater understanding. Students probably do not need to read about theory or methodology before jumping into the experience, but they do need—as do faculty—to read texts related to the site they are studying.

The second step in planning an active-learning experience is scheduling experts. When to schedule meetings with experts within the structure of the learning experience depends on individual circumstances except for one general principle: do not place them at the beginning. The students need to have a chance to formulate their own ideas before testing them against expert opinions. Ideally the experts enter into conversation with the students, so the students need to have something to say in order to be active participants in the discussion rather than passive listeners.

What follows are some examples of (1) texts assigned as readings and (2) experts scheduled in Faculty Institutes at three sites.

Faculty Institute on "Exploring Blues Terrains" in Memphis and the Mississippi Delta

Readings:

- *Junior Ray*, John Pritchard, 2005. (a novel from the point of view of a Mississippi "good ole boy" that raises issues about race and class with an unusual slant, thus provoking questions about the South and its historical and current culture)

- "The Blues Is Something from the Heart," Big Bill Broonzy, Memphis Slim, and Sonny Boy Williamson. (the 1940s musings of three blues greats on the meaning of their music)

- "Down to the Crossroads," Mark Jacobson, *Natural History* 105.9 (Sept. 1996). (a narrative about the geography, ethnography, and history of the Delta)

- "What is the Blues?" chapter 1 of *Escaping the Delta* (2005). (a debunking of myths about the meaning and structure of blues music, the perception of blues musicians, and everything else about the Delta)

- "Introduction," *Forgotten Time: The Yazoo-Mississippi Delta after the Civil War* (University of Virginia Press, 2000). (a history of the Delta and its relationship to the South before and after the Civil War, including who lived there, who owned it, and the present and past state of race relations)

- Blues Lyrics: *Beale Street Blues, Got My Mojo Working, Backlash Blues, Memphis Blues*

Experts:

- John Pritchard (author of *Junior Ray*)
- Johnnie Billington (blues guitarist)
- Bobby "Blue" Bland (blues and soul singer)
- Curator of the Delta Blues Museum

Faculty Institute on "New Orleans: Recovery/Discovery"

Readings:

- *Place as Text*, ed. Bernice Braid and Ada Long (2000)
- *Why New Orleans Matters*, Tom Piazza (2005)

Film:

- *When the Levees Broke: Requiem in Fours Acts*, Spike Lee (2006)

Experts:

- Lance Hill, Director, Southern Institute for Educational Research

- Loretta Pyles, Assistant Professor of Social Work, Tulane University
- Wilmer Brown, Pastor, Central Congregational Church
- Ali Arnold, Retained Instructor, UNO; Director & Principal Dancer, N.O.madic Tribal
- Lolis Eric Elie, Columnist, *Times-Picayune*
- David Good, Cardiology Fellow, Ochsner Clinic

Faculty Institute on "A Tale of Two Cities: Minneapolis & St. Paul / Identity & Assimilation"

Readings:

- *Place as Text*
- "Simultaneous Perception" from *The Experience of Place* by Tony Hiss
- "Riverside on the Rise" (*Walljasper*)
- "On the Job, Their Way" (*Star Tribune*)
- "The Ice Palace" (from F. Scott Fitzgerald's *St. Paul Stories*)
- From *Little* by David Treuer
- *Twin Cities Noir* edited by Schaper and Horwitz (focus on stories from the following neighborhoods: Frogtown, Near North, Uptown, Cedar-Riverside, West 7th-Fort Road, Downtown Minneapolis, Summit-University, Downtown St. Paul)

Experts:

- Park rangers, social service providers, librarians, and other local resources with whom participants conferred during their field explorations

These three examples of readings and experts illustrate different tactics appropriate to the sites, themes, and purposes of three

29

particular Faculty Institutes. In Memphis, where the focus was the interrelationship between music and place, the readings included short pieces of and about the blues that privileged downhome insights over musicology. Some brief and more academic pieces focused on the nature of the region, and the readings included an offbeat novel about the Delta by a local writer, who met with the group several times as they traveled in and around Memphis; this Institute included considerable time on the road traveling through the often bleak countryside and small, impoverished towns. The two main experts were practitioners of the blues who described and demonstrated blues history and techniques that the group also experienced at local blues clubs. The Curator of the Delta Blues Museum gave a more academic overview only toward the end of the Institute, which was designed above all to give participants a feel for the place, for its music, and for the interconnections between them.

The focus in New Orleans was less on the arts or on the feel of the place than on understanding the recent catastrophe of Katrina in relation to the unique culture and demography of this city, and so the assigned reading was a book of cultural analysis that prepared participants to understand the context of what had occurred there as well as its implications for the rest of the country. The experts, who started meeting with participants after their initial explorations of the storm-damaged and often desolate neighborhoods outside of the French Quarter, included people from different parts of New Orleans culture who had had direct experience of Katrina, including a doctor, a journalist, a performance artist, and a pastor as well as two academics. The overview of Tom Piazza's book provided an important anchor for the Institute, and the perspectives of people who endured Katrina as well as the all-important discussions among participants brought essential focus to this emotionally charged Institute.

Finally, the Minneapolis/St. Paul Institute had a more traditional focus on urban studies: participants compared the two cities with their different levels of cultural diversity, affluence, and civic pride. The readings did not include the standard readings from, say, Jane Jacobs or William H. Whyte but instead were primarily fictional and journalistic pieces, and the experts were ordinary workers in the city such as social service providers and park rangers. Participants discovered through their growing awareness of the fundamental differences between the two neighboring cities many of the basic issues and principles of urban development and planning, with the facilitators at the end providing theoretical perspectives that connected what they had observed to what urban historians had postulated.

What the three examples indicate is that context dictates the character of both readings and experts, but in all cases the direct experiences of participants in Faculty Institutes are primary. The readings and experts enhance without dominating the voices of the participants, who glean understanding and authority from truths that, as Dickinson suggests, "dazzle gradually" in the experience of any particular place and its people.

REFERENCES

Braid, Bernice and Ada Long, eds. *Place as Text: Approaches to Active Learning*. Lincoln, NE: National Collegiate Honors Council, 2000. NCHC Monograph Series. Print.

—. *Place as Text: Approaches to Active Learning*. 2nd ed. Lincoln, NE: National Collegiate Honors Council, 2010. NCHC Monograph Series. Print.

Dickinson, Emily. "Tell all the Truth but tell it slant—" (#1129). *The Norton Anthology of Poetry*. Eds. Arthur M. Eastman et al. New York: Norton, 1970. 855–56. Print.

"Essential Knowledge: Baedeker Guides." AbeBooks.com, courtesy of Rarebookreview. <http://www.abebooks.com/docs/Community/Featured/RBR/baedekers.shtml>.

Frommer, Arthur. *Europe on 5 Dollars a Day*. Reproduction of original 1957 edition. New York: Frommer's, 2007. Print.

James, Henry. *Portraits of Places*. Cambridge, MA: Cambridge UP, 2009. Cambridge Library Collection. Digital Print.

Kolb, David A. *Experiential Learning: Experience as the Source of Learning and Development.* Englewood Cliffs, NJ: Prentice-Hall, 1984. Print.

Machonis, Peter, ed. *Shatter the Glassy Stare: Implementing Experiential Learning in Higher Education.* Lincoln: National Collegiate Honors Council, 2008. NCHC Monograph Series. Print.

Mack, Doug. *Europe on 5 Wrong Turns a Day: One Man, Eight Countries, One Vintage Travel Guide.* New York: Penguin Books, 2012. Perigree Trade Books. Print.

Twain, Mark. *A Tramp Abroad.* Ch. XXXIX. New York: Penguin Classics, 1997. Print.

CHAPTER 4

The Beginner's Mind:
Recursive Writing in NCHC Faculty Institutes

Sara E. Quay

While the majority of essays in this volume focus on how writing can enhance experiential learning for college students, one of the major challenges to such initiatives is the faculty. As Ada Long writes, "Active learning . . . makes unfamiliar demands on teachers" (25). Trained as experts, faculty members must remember how to step away from that role and, as Bernice Braid says, join students as "co-participants and co-investigators" (6). Accustomed to providing authoritative readings and being experts on course content, teachers may be uncomfortable, writes Long, when asked to adopt the "unnerving" idea of "trusting others to come to insights and wisdom and truths on their own" (24, 25). Familiar with the canon of tried-and-true assignments, teachers may also resist what Robyn S. Martin describes as the creation and implementation of a brand new, untested, course-long assignment. If any of the ideas offered in this collection are to be effective for students, however, faculty must make changes to the very nature of their craft. Based

33

on the principles of City as Text™, NCHC Faculty Institutes and in particular their recursive writing assignments are one way to meet the goal of pedagogical innovation.

Faculty Institutes offer a unique opportunity for faculty to return to a position that is the diametrecal opposite of the academic expert, namely to a beginner's mind. In doing so, faculty have the opportunity to remember what it is like not to know, to feel lost, to "begin again," as Gladys Palma de Schrynemakers suggests (99). Sponsored by the NCHC Honors Semesters Committee, Faculty Institutes provide professional development opportunities for faculty "who want to acquire greater familiarity with design elements of CAT as a learning strategy, and who are considering applying these field explorations either to their own campus courses/programs or for use in international study" ("Faculty Institutes"). Institutes are compressed courses on CAT and use strategies described in other essays—walkabouts, interviews, jottings, observations—to engage learners in the world around them. The first Faculty Institute I participated in was provocatively titled "Death and Desire in the American West: Las Vegas and Death Valley." Although I did not know exactly what to expect when I signed up, the Institute changed my thinking about not only the specific places that were the focus of the Institute but my teaching as well.

What differentiates Faculty Institutes from other experiential-learning opportunities is the three-assignment writing sequence completed over the course of a four- to seven-day Institute. Similar to the writing students do in Honors Semesters, the Faculty Institute sequence, according to Braid, aims "to record observations and details in context; to interpret, analyze and substantiate these details; and to uncover the observers' perspective on both what they were viewing and their own way of seeing" (5). For faculty in particular, who are used to being in the knowledge-granting role of an expert, each piece of writing is an invitation to remember what it is like not to know, to make sense of new information, to synthesize diverse perspectives, and to witness their own learning process. Participants complete three types of recursive writing assignments during a Faculty Institute. Some assignments are completed more than once, depending on the length and setting of the Institute, but the sequence is critical in the process of allowing faculty to return again to the place of being learners.

FIRST IMPRESSIONS ASSIGNMENT

The initial Faculty Institute writing assignment is a First Impressions piece that takes place the opening night of any Institute. Institutes typically begin in the early afternoon with a group meeting from which participants are directly sent out in small groups to explore different parts of the immediate vicinity around the hotel or lodging. Called a "walkabout," this two- or three-hour excursion is an opportunity for participants to collect their preliminary ideas about the place: Who lives and works there? How do you know? How is space being used? Are there stores or homes in the area? What are they like? Who seems to use them? Sometimes a more focused prompt will be included in the brief directions for the walkabout, asking participants to focus on the theme of "private use of public space," but overall the idea is to send people into the area to observe the local environment in detail.

While the walkabout itself catapults experienced faculty out of the comfortable role of the expert and back to the role of the beginner, the First Impressions writing assignment asks Institute participants to record their experience in words. After a debriefing meeting during which participants share their experiences of the afternoon, they receive their first writing assignment: write an informal piece about initial impressions collected that day. Participants often experience some anxiety in response to this request: How long should the piece be? What should it focus on? What if it is not done on time?

Because of the transformation of faculty back into the role of students, the prospect of writing, especially writing not as an expert in their field but as observers of their own experience, can be challenging. Used to wielding discipline-based jargon and academic language with ease, writers of First Impressions often struggle for language to describe new information and encounter "the inadequacy of words and my feelings of clumsiness in summoning them," as John Major says about his first Honors Semester essay at Long Island University (15). In addition, the debriefing discussion asks participants to hear different perspectives on the site being explored, and that diversity of voices is further de-centering as participants consider not just their own experience but the experiences of others. That process lays the foundation for the second writing assignment.

OBSERVATIONS ASSIGNMENT

Participants complete the second writing assignment for a Faculty Institute after a full day of explorations. Once again participants are sent in small groups to different destinations with some questions to consider along the way. In what is usually an all-day excursion, participants venture farther afield than in the initial walkabout, and they seek more detailed observations and engagement with the place and people. This exploration is an opportunity to deepen the initial impressions gathered in the first walkabout and to begin to integrate new knowledge into a growing understanding of place.

Reflecting the longer length of time and deeper exploration required during this day, the Observations writing assignment asks participants for another level of writing. While writers may return to, revise, and build on the themes and ideas of their first assignment, evidence, as well as impressions from the day's exploration, is an important part of this second piece of writing. They use interviews with people encountered during the day to support, retract, or refine an initial impression. Details observed and documented, witnessed and confirmed, create more concrete ways to describe the place. Information gathered from the prior evening's discussion—where numerous voices came together to share different perspectives—can also be tested or affirmed by the day's exploration.

This writing goes beyond the surface by capturing a deeper, more concrete understanding of the place—patterns, contradictions, behaviors, and beliefs—that make the city or town or landscape what it is. The writing, therefore, is more integrative, supporting claims with evidence gathered during the day's outing. For faculty used to writing arguments based on a familiar field of study, this assignment reminds them of what it is like to develop claims about new knowledge and to make these claims based on experiential evidence as well as conversations with peers who may or may not view things in the same way. Such writing reminds faculty how much is at stake in making a claim, how fragile these claims are even as the evidence mounts to support them, and, perhaps most importantly, how making claims can place writers in dialogue with others whose perspectives may or may not be in keeping with their own.

TURNING POINT ESSAY

The final and culminating writing assignment of a Faculty Institute is the Turning Point essay. Just as Honors Semesters students like John Major produce written reflections on a pivotal moment (or moments) in their experience, so do participants in Faculty Institutes. The goal of the Turning Point essay, Braid writes, is for writers to record their "own evolution over time, identifying which specific event was a catalyst for what they see as a change in their ways of knowing" (11). The power of these essays, she emphasizes, lies in the way they "furnish instrumentality to explorers engaged in making sense of the radically new, unfiltered information that field experiences plunge them into" (10–11). In other words, when faculty members write a Turning Point essay, they are shifting the spotlight onto themselves, their own learning, and the way that learning changes them.

The prompt for a Turning Point essay generally asks the writer to describe a specific scene, event, or discussion that led to a shift in perspective or a new insight that arose over the course of the Institute. It is not just a descriptive essay, however. The writer's work is to identify the turning point—whatever it may be—and to reflect on the elements that provoked the change. This type of writing moves beyond the initial jottings of the First Impressions assignment even as it refers back to the sense of disorientation and new perspectives often captured in that early piece of writing. Unlike the Observations assignment, which is in some ways a revision of the

First Impressions and more academic in its efforts to make sense of the participants' experiences, the Turning Point essay is highly personal. At the same time, Turning Point essays also build on the Observations assignment in that they ask writers to make claims about themselves—a moment that shifted their perspective—and to dig deeper into the process that facilitated or allowed that change to occur.

As the culminating piece in the three-assignment writing sequence, the Turning Point essay offers faculty the opportunity to reflect both personally and professionally on their experience as learners. In examining shifts in their perspectives and understanding over the course of the Institute, where they have been learners engaged in a new environment, participants begin to see the way that their teaching can shift as well. I wrote at the end of my Turning Point essay in the Las Vegas/Death Valley Institute:

> I am beginning to see how writing other than academic papers can focus the process and how giving students the frame but letting them paint the picture will enrich their learning and my teaching. I see how the process is at least as important as the product and that my job is to send students out to explore and then listen to and engage with them when they return. I understand that there are places in my courses that can be altered to meet these goals more effectively. . . . I also have been invigorated by doing the walkabouts and explorations myself—not just teaching about them but doing them has re-engaged me with the excitement of observing, talking, interviewing, and organizing information. (109–10)

These thoughts on my teaching did not come about without repeated reflection on my own learning over the course of the Institute. It was my exploration of a new place, my deepening understanding of that place through interviews, observations, and discussion, and finally my documentation and analysis of the process in writing that ultimately allowed me to return to my teaching with a fresh perspective, a beginner's mind. For those wishing to do the same, the writing sequence at the heart of a Faculty Institute may just do the trick.

REFERENCES

Braid, Bernice. "History and Theory of Recursive Writing in Experiential Education." *Writing on Your Feet: Reflective Practices in City as Text*™. Ed. Ada Long. Lincoln: National Collegiate Honors Council, 2014. 3–12. NCHC Monograph Series. Print.

de Schrynemakers, Gladys Palma. "Experiential Learning, Reflective Writing, and Civic Dialogue: Keeping Democracy on its Feet." *Writing on Your Feet: Reflective Practices in City as Text*™. Ed. Ada Long. Lincoln: National Collegiate Honors Council, 2014. 93–100. NCHC Monograph Series. Print.

"Faculty Institutes." *nchchonors.org.* National Collegiate Honors Council, n.d. Web. 30 March 2013.

Long, Ada. "The Role of Background Readings and Experts." *Writing on Your Feet: Reflective Practices in City as Text*™. Ed. Ada Long. Lincoln: National Collegiate Honors Council, 2014. 23–32. NCHC Monograph Series. Print.

Major, John. "Claiming a Voice through Writing." *Writing on Your Feet: Reflective Practices in City as Text*™. Ed. Ada Long. Lincoln: National Collegiate Honors Council, 2014. 13–21. NCHC Monograph Series. Print.

Martin, Robyn S. "Finding Appropriate Assignments: Mapping an Honors Semester." *Writing on Your Feet: Reflective Practices in City as Text*™. Ed. Ada Long. Lincoln: National Collegiate Honors Council, 2014. 57–62. NCHC Monograph Series. Print.

Quay, Sara E. "Death and Desire in the American West: Las Vegas/Death Valley." *Writing on Your Feet: Reflective Practices in City as Text*™. Ed. Ada Long. Lincoln: National Collegiate Honors Council, 2014. 103–10. NCHC Monograph Series. Print.

CHAPTER 5

Assigning, Analyzing, and Assessing Recursive Writing in Honors Semesters

Ann Raia

People often think of reflective writing as a solitary activity, an ordered reconstruction of past thoughts and activities, the stuff of diaries and memoirs, well removed from life and action, uncontested in its perspective, a fixed snapshot of events past and inert. Reflection is a mental activity rarely prized in American culture, where people do little of it in their daily lives, acting instead on first impressions, instincts, and assumptions. Americans often see reflective writing as an activity of the elderly, authoritative thoughts shared with those less experienced who were not directly involved in the action described. Reflective writing about shared experience, however, has a developmental role to play in academia, where the exchange of such writing within a community of peers can deepen learning, foster self-assessment, and correct the myopia of single vision.

Having observed the effect of reflective writing as both a leader and participant in City as Text™, in Faculty Institutes, on the Honors

41

Semesters Planning Committee, and in Honors Semesters in various capacities as Program Director, Facilitator of Directed Study, and Evaluator, I believe that it has a powerful capacity for what I can only describe as moral development. While the writing process in Honors Semesters is designed to move participants away from dualistic thinking and reactions based on stereotypes, it also precipitates a broadening of perception and attitude that the eminent American psychologist Abraham Maslow (1908–1970) defined as the highest level of motivation in his theory of the hierarchy of needs. In his original five-step model, he posited that humans are motivated at the first level to obtain the basic necessities required for their survival. Once this first set of needs is satisfied, higher needs emerge for security through order and law, then for love and for affiliation with a group, then for esteem through recognition or achievement, and then finally for self-actualization, the fulfillment of personal potential. Later in his professional life, Maslow saw evidence of another step beyond self-actualization that he termed "transhumanistic," a motivational need for self-transcendence characterized by altruistic action or a sense of identity extending outside the boundaries of self (qtd. in Koltko-Rivera 303).

In the New York City Honors Semester "Media & Image: Issues of Gender and Work" (fall of 1996), reflective writing assignments realized a number of goals related to the higher steps of Maslow's hierarchy of needs, including self-actualization, group affiliation, and self-transcendence. The opportunity for students to share perspectives in open discussion, to foster a community of experiential learners, and to stretch their sense of identity was especially important. The demographics and interests of participants in the Honors Semester rendered these goals both essential and challenging. The students came from twenty-five different schools (large and small, public and private) in eighteen different states, the majority being small-town dwellers unfamiliar with New York City. They also reported a broad spectrum of major fields from ceramic engineering to philosophy and expressed interests that were split equally between the two themes of media/internship and gender/women's studies.

WRITING ASSIGNMENTS IN THE 1996 NEW YORK CITY HONORS SEMESTER

Starting in Orientation Week, the writing assignments followed the model of City as Text, aiming for development of critical and self-reflective thinking. These first assignments communicated faculty expectations for the semester, and students' essays provided important initial feedback but were not graded in a traditional manner. Since honors students can be expected to write at a college level but also to be over-anxious about grades, the first assignments received numerical evaluations that showed students where they stood but that clearly would not count in a final grade. Two seminar teachers wrote specific comments on each text, and all students were given the option of revision and faculty reevaluation. Roxanne Zimmer, who taught Communication, Work, and Gender, and Barbara McManus, who taught The Lenses of Gender, collaborated to create and evaluate the two City as Text essays that they assigned during Orientation. The reflective writing assignments continued in McManus's seminar, where students used their theoretical readings and activities to give meaning to the semester's experiences and to test their textual understanding in public conversation. These assignments counted for forty percent of the final grade.

The writing requirements for the core seminar were as follows:

Papers: All papers should be word processed (single-spaced with a double space between paragraphs, 1" margins all around, signed on the back of the final page). Any sources used should be properly cited and documented according to a standard format (MLA, APA, etc.). More detailed instructions for each paper will be provided in the Schedule of Topics and Assignments.

Orientation Week: *City as Text: Destinations* (due September 8) and *City as Text: Private Use of Public Space* (due September 10). Evaluated.

Turning Point Essay #1: *City as Text:Becoming a Participant/ Observer* (due September 16). Reflection on the significance of the participant/observation exercises in New York City. Maximum length 5 pages; graded. Discussion/workshop on Turning Point Essay #1.

Turning Point Essay #2: *Work as Text: Applying and Testing Theory* (due October 15). Critical analysis of the internship work site using theoretical frameworks studied in class. Maximum 7 pages; graded. Discussion/workshop on Turning Point Essay #2.

Vision Paper: *Where Do We Go from Here?* (due December 3). Projection of changes desired for the future and of strategies for accomplishing these changes. Maximum 5 pages; graded.

The more detailed descriptions of the two Turning Point essays were as follows:

Turning Point Essay #1:
City as Text: Becoming a Participant/Observer.

Instructions: This 5-page essay has three parts, all of which involve *personal reflection* on your experiences of the first week, particularly your "City as Text" visits to New York City (but you may also include other experiences of NYC during this time). Do not repeat narratives and descriptions already written and handed in; instead, *reflect on* and *analyze* the significance of these experiences with the perspective of hindsight. This is indeed a *turning point*: you are now embarking on the internships and coursework that will theorize and concretize your living/working/learning for the semester. This assignment gives you a chance to look back over the admittedly jam-packed (not to mention hot and humid) activities that launched this semester and to ponder what you have learned. In your first two written assignments, you tended to emphasize narrative and description (*what* happened, *what* you did, *what* you saw); now is your chance to decide what it all means and *why* it is significant. Please be specific and concrete; back up your statements with details and examples.

Part 1—process: Describe and analyze your response to the experience of becoming a participant/observer. Do you agree with Emerson, Fretz, and Shaw (*Writing Ethnographic Fieldnotes*, p. 15) that this type of writing "helps the field researcher to understand what he has been observing in the first place and, thus, enables him to participate in new ways, to hear with greater acuteness, and to observe with a new lens"? If so, why? If not, why not?

Part 2—site: Compare your actual experience of New York City with your preconceptions of the city. What assumptions have your experiences confirmed; what assumptions have they challenged? Do you think this interaction with NYC has been valuable? Why or why not?

Part 3—lens: Describe and analyze your reaction to the experience of interpreting incidents from the perspective of gender. Did you observe/write anything about gender in your two papers? Why or why not? Do you think this is an important perspective to use in the context of participant/observer exercises? Why or why not?

**Turning Point Essay #2: Work as Text:
Applying and Testing Theory**.

Instructions: This 7-page essay is the most concentrated critical essay you will write in this course, so make the most of it. This essay involves both observation/description and theoretical analysis as applied in particular to your internship experiences. Both should be present, but the weight should fall on the application of theory. Cite and document all sources according to an accepted format (MLA, APA, etc.). The following two questions do not have to be answered in separate parts of the paper; indeed, integration of the two is likely to produce a more coherent essay.

1. Describe your work site as a "gendered workplace," including such matters as ranges and types of leadership displayed by management and co-workers; gender differences in interpersonal interactions (how are you treated by managers and co-workers? how do individuals in these groups treat each other?); awareness of gender issues among management and co-workers; questions of authority and responsibility. Assume that the reader knows nothing about your work site; be sure to give enough basic information in terms of sex ratios, type of work performed, etc. Personal names may be omitted or changed if desired.

2. Analyze these individual situations in the light of the theoretical models we have studied (i.e., use theory to critique your experience and use your experience to evaluate the theories in terms of validity and usefulness). When applying the theories, you may, if you wish, supplement your internship experiences with other workplace experiences to provide concrete examples.

A CASE STUDY OF STUDENT WRITING

One student in the Honors Semester, Jack Walsh, has happily given permission to discuss his work as a case study of the process students go through in an Honors Semester. In his self-introduction to the Honors Semester community for the first meeting, Walsh wrote:

Jack Walsh, a native of Canton, North Carolina, is a junior Mass Communication major at the University of North Carolina-Asheville. A dean's list student, he spent this past summer studying at St. Benet's Hall in Oxford, England. He has been active with the UNCA *Blue Banner* newspaper staff, the Haywood Arts Repertory Theatre, and Food Not Bombs. An amateur guitarist/songwriter in his spare time, Jack, judging by his current rate of musical progress, plans to stay an amateur for a good while.

For the first Turning Point assignment called "City as Text: Becoming a Participant//Observer," students were asked to rethink their Orientation week experiences of New York City and to use their two observation narratives ("what happened, what you did, what you saw") as notes for the essay, reflecting on and analyzing them for meaning and giving "specific and concrete" examples. For his observations, Walsh was assigned to the Murray Hill section of Manhattan and Chinatown even though he would have preferred Greenwich Village and 52nd Street. His Turning Point essay, just over three pages long, opens with his identifying himself as "an ethnographer." He is self-conscious about his writing: "I tend to labor over everything I write. Striving for just the right words, I complicate even the simplest plot summaries." He confesses that, had he not had the guidance of the observation assignments, he would have "just wandered aimlessly, not really thinking about what I saw."

On his walkabouts Walsh found nothing at first to write about, but when he returned for a second look, he saw an interesting scene through an open door to an Italian men's club. Citing concern for his observer status ("I didn't want to interfere with the continuity of my surroundings"), he chose not to enter. Walsh recognized and was sensitive to his outsider status. While noting the oddity of street life and seeking to be a part of "the normal NY scheme of things," he realized that only "non-locals" would pay attention to what he was finding unusual; "for Manhattaners who have seen it all, abnormality seemed to be the norm." He saw that only someone who knew the city was able, "as Emerson, Fretz, and Shaw put it, to participate in new ways, to hear with greater acuteness, & to observe with a new lens" and that he was "often struggling to find a reference point."

Unlike the perceptions by those more familiar with the city, Walsh's views were shaped by encyclopedia facts, romantic Frank Sinatra ballads, and the Christian family tours of his childhood. The New York of "disgusting opulence and appalling poverty" was not in evidence in the areas he was assigned to, but he wondered about the well-dressed people leisurely strolling from store to store on a Thursday mid-afternoon with shopping bags from the Gap, Macy's, and Virgin Megastore. He did not find New Yorkers rude but "rather impersonal"; "it's just as it is in any big city."

While Walsh found the racial and cultural dynamics of New York "initially more obvious and interesting," he looked harder and realized that "because I did not readily notice the gender dynamics of the parts of New York I explored, I can assume that it is often easy to ignore such issues." Adopting the perspective of gender as he had been instructed, he found some examples in the street life he was observing and then turned the lens inward "to examine just how it shapes my own interactions with others." Walsh concluded that, once he had been in the city a while, it would "be interesting to reexamine my observations and see the city with a new lens all over again."

The second Turning Point assignment, on "Work as Text: Applying and Testing Theory," asked students to reflect through the lenses of gender on their observations during the four weeks at their internship sites. The assignment advised students to apply both observation/description and theoretical analysis to their internship experiences, with the emphasis on theory. This assignment was due six weeks into the semester, a month after the first Turning Point essay and after students in the course Lenses of Gender had read and discussed materials, viewed videos, engaged in simulations, and attended a lecture by a vice president of a telecommunications firm about sexual harassment. Walsh, like most students who came to the Honors Semester, was attracted by the opportunity to have a New York City internship, but, unlike the others, he was not skeptical about gender theory and practice even though he had never studied it before. However, all of the students—in applying theoretical analysis of seminar readings to their observations and in describing situations from their internship experiences—discovered realities of the "gendered workplace" that they had never noticed before.

Walsh's Directed Study for the Honors Semester was "Oh, Lady Be Good: Women in the New York Jazz Scene," for which he made a video that he presented at the end-of-semester colloquium; he also participated in a Round Table discussion on "The New York Scene." Walsh's internship was at BioMedia, Inc., working with the executive producer, who was also his second reader. An excerpt from his abstract for the colloquium program demonstrates his personal integration of the Honors Semester themes and advocacy for equality.

> While this project was conceived out of an interest in jazz, it has come to serve as an illustration of gender dynamics in the arts and in the workplace. As the future of jazz becomes uncertain due to low record sales and what many critics believe to be lower artistic standards, this project implies that perhaps critics, record producers, and club owners should pay attention to women in the New York jazz scene, for they too have much to contribute.

Walsh's integration of his New York experiences extends beyond the Honors Semester into his subsequent career and life. He is now a producer/editor at the PBS affiliate Public Broadcasting Atlanta. His programs have won seven regional Emmy Awards, an additional ten Emmy nominations, more than fifteen Telly Awards, and a Georgia Association of Broadcasters' Gabby Award. He is currently finishing work on the documentary *Cosplay: Crafting a Secret Identity,* a follow-up to the Emmy-winning *Four Days at Dragon*Con,* which was picked up for national distribution by American Public Television. He also writes about pop culture for the website *Scene Missing Magazine* <http://scenemissingmagazine.com> and gives guest lectures on video anthropology at Davidson College.

ASSESSMENT OF REFLECTIVE WRITING

Assessment of reflective writing in Honors Semesters is a complex affair. By necessity, a faculty expert must award a grade on a standard scale because grades are the language that students have been trained to understand, registrars can enter on transcripts, and academicians value. Far more important to writing in the Honors Semesters, however, is the process of review that includes faculty critique, to be sure, but stresses presentation of texts anonymously for open discussion within a community of peers, followed by not just revision but a return to the writing in another context. Traditionally, the assessment of student writing is a well-kept secret between a shamed or gloating author and a faculty member whose judgment is not to be questioned; such assessment has no after-life except as a component of the final grade. Reflective writing has a different kind of authorial weight such that a faculty member can assess the *logos* of a text (evidence, assumptions, and conclusions) in the same way as traditional academic papers while the *ethos* and *pathos* require a different—preferably collective and reciprocal—kind of evaluation. The personality and character of the writer—rooted in a distinct geographical, social, ethnic, spiritual, and cultural background—inform reflective writing in ways that defy rubrics or standardization. Group discussion and analysis are ideal in generating an evaluative discourse that is useful to both the writer and the evaluators. When reflective writing becomes a text for analysis and thoughtful discussion, the author, faculty, and fellow students are all engaged in the process of mutual understanding and inspiration.

Assessment begins with the creation and articulation of the reflective writing assignment. The facilitator sets up a careful process that gives clear and specific direction to student experience and writing. Where do you want them to go? What do you want them to do? What attitudes do you want them to adopt? What should they focus on? What models of behavior do you offer them? What resources are they to use? What modes of critical thinking will you look for in their papers? More tediously, how long should the essay be, and what format should they use?

While the assignment needs to set forth precise expectations, feedback should be comprehensive and prompt, based on evaluation criteria that have been made public and that correspond fairly to the assigned exercise. Giving a letter grade is not always necessary, but written commentary on the text is imperative. In some circumstances, offering the possibility for revision and re-evaluation will be beneficial for promoting student understanding, and faculty re-evaluation of revisions is a precious gift. Some consider revision an unfair advantage to the student who rewrites, but this objection seems unwarranted if the option is open to everyone. Revisiting a text is always productive for an author, especially after class discussion of the assignment, but it does not always satisfy the desire for an A; the several students in the New York Semester who took advantage of the option to revise had B grades that rose only slightly.

Part of what one looks for in assessing reflective writing, especially among honors students, is coherence of argument and clarity of expression. One looks also for responsiveness to the assignment and for full and serious treatment of all its parts without verbosity. On the level of content, one seeks a narrative of significant ideas and observations through description, analysis, comparison, and interpretation. Finally, since issues of attitude matter in this kind of writing, the author should demonstrate honesty, openness, and willingness to move beyond assumptions, preconceptions, and stereotypes.

For example, in response to his first Turning Point essay, McManus gave Jack Walsh an A. In her verbal evaluation, she commended him for "a very perceptive and thoughtful essay, conveying a real effort to carry out the assignment's focus on reflection and 'pondering what it all means.'" She added, "You use pertinent examples and nicely present details to explain and illustrate your points, and you express your reservations cogently." Furthermore, she said, Walsh's essay demonstrated his sensitivity as an outsider to being intrusive, his questioning of the validity of an Emerson quotation he was asked to consider, his rueful review of childhood memories of New York City, his confirmation and rejection of clichés about the city through fresh observation, and his willingness to apply unfamiliar gender perspectives to what he saw and to his personal interactions. Walsh's essay showed that he not only mentally revisited his earlier field experiences and written observations but was committed to revisiting them again.

By the end of the semester, faculty members were ready to ask students to become assessors. Zimmer asked the students in her internship seminar to write a final Turning Point essay reviewing their experiences—academic, social, and personal—throughout the semester. The exercise was not graded because it encouraged students to take stock, to use their new critical writing tools to reflect on three months of personal engagement with the semester's themes of work, gender, community, and identity. In their response to this writing assignment, far more than in the formal end-of-semester evaluations that most students did not complete, they spoke to their deep experience of personal change and of taking responsibility for the new person they had become. The responses evidenced a sense of accomplishment, confidence, empowerment, reordered priorities, new habits of thinking, and not just a willingness but a sense of duty to speak up and out. Many of them showed signs of having attained a higher level of personal motivation and of what Maslow called self-actualization. Quotations from the final Turning Point essays provide some sense of this personal transformation:

- Perhaps . . . what I leave behind is the most important thing. I leave behind a negative attitude, intolerance, doubts about my future, indifference about gender issues, and my misconceptions about New York. No longer will these obscure my perceived realities.

- This semester has taught me so many things that I do not know how to put them all together, but I think that is the beauty of the whole experience. I have grown and changed and feel more comfortable with my own identity. Now I only have one mask to form and wear, my own. Instead of feeling sad because the semester is ending, I am excited. I am ready to explore more of the world around me.

- On a professional level, I must say that I did learn a lot at my internship at MTV, even though I no longer really want to work there. I realized what it is MTV actually does in terms of what they produce, how they do it, and how they maintain their high profit margins: very basic, rather monotonous programs, in a pretty basic, monotonous way, and by categorizing most employees as freelancers so they don't have to give them benefits. Although my internship may not have been as positive of an experience as I had hoped it would have been, the knowledge and awareness that I gained outweigh any negative aspects that I experienced.

- The semester has given me focus for my future. It has allowed me to weed out the skills that I can use to my advantage and the ones that I need to continue working on. I came with the notion that I wanted to spend my internship time hob-nobbing around a huge lush corporate environment, dressed in expensive suits and lace camisoles, and work my way to the top. Now I know I want no part of that. If the corporate world is going to force me to turn into one of the people I work with, I want no part of it. Many of them have to give up their morals, hopes of having a family, and ability to lead their own lives. I want to be able to use and experience my life to its fullest. I want to be in control of my decisions and be thrown as many challenges as possible.

- It's been extremely heartening to see this many people my age who have very strong views about feminism, about equality, about societal roles and expectations. It's a great experience to be able to bounce my ideas off of other people, have them critiqued, sharpened. Good things almost always come when you are forced to think, to defend something you think you believe. Thoughtful discussions can answer questions that reading or studying alone cannot.

Finally, this poem by one of the students distinctively captures the sense of personal change and ownership that a majority of the students laid claim to in their writing at the close of the Honors Semester:

What did I learn? A short list.
I can go places: I am decent
I am tough, but not that tough
I am patient, but not
I am not a butt kisser
I am not a networker
I am not that ambitious
I want to be good at what I do
I want to learn: I love to learn
I am tired of jumping through hoops for grades

I am ready to work
I want children and a home
Family and friends outweigh a job
You can write anywhere: everything is interesting

If only one student had learned that "You can write anywhere" and that "everything is interesting," the Honors Semester would have been a success, but this outcome seemed to characterize the life-changing destination toward which students journeyed during and after the semester. Not all of the students engaged as fully in their reflective writing assignments as faculty would have liked, but all discovered clearer vision from trying on new lenses and new critical voices while sharing their reflective writing in communal discussion with faculty and colleagues. While not all gave voice to personal epiphanies at the time, such revelations typically occur after an Honors Semester when the students return home to familiar environments and apply the approaches they learned during the semester, seeing their home and campus cultures with new eyes.

The students were not alone in experiencing conversions during and after the Honors Semester. The three faculty members who collaborated with the students in the semester-long seminars and also the resident director discovered in the reflective writing process an opportunity for shared thinking and learning, an experience of what good education—the "leading out" of the heart and mind—could and should be. Notes they received from alumni as well as conversations with colleagues suggested that the New York City Honors Semester had led both students and faculty toward Maslow's "transhumanistic" ideal, an extension of and beyond the self, which emerged in large part through the recursive practice of reflective writing (qtd. in Koltko-Rivera 303).

REFERENCES

Emerson, Robert M., Rachel I. Fretz, and Linda L. Shaw. *Writing Ethnographic Fieldnotes*. Chicago: U of Chicago P, 1995. Print.

Koltko-Rivera, Mark E.. "Rediscovering the Later Version of Maslow's Hierarchy of Needs: Self-Transcendence and Opportunities for Theory, Research, and Unification." *Review of General Psychology* 10.4 (2006): 302–17. Print.

CHAPTER 6

Finding Appropriate Assignments: Mapping an Honors Semester

Robyn S. Martin

[Editor's note: This chapter is a reprint of an essay entitled "Mapping a Semester: Using Cultural Mapping in an Honors Humanities Course" published in Honors in Practice 9 (2013): *69–72.]*

On a bright August day in 2012, a select group of honors students and a small group of faculty gathered in a classroom at Northern Arizona University. Most of us were strangers to each other. Certainly none of the students, who traveled from other universities around the country, knew each other, yet we were all soon to become a tight-knit group devoted to an entire semester of place-based, experiential learning. That late summer day marked the beginning of orientation for the Grand Canyon Semester (GCS), the third to be offered jointly by the National Collegiate Honors Council (NCHC) and Northern Arizona University (NAU).

Grand Canyon Semesters are integrated learning experiences in the humanities and sciences. Students study the environmental and social challenges confronting us in the twenty-first century using an interdisciplinary approach to the curriculum. During previous semesters, participants have tackled complex issues such as how to balance environmental protection of Grand Canyon National Park while still meeting the needs of over five million visitors each year. Past GCS students have also, in an outdoor classroom experience, excavated and stabilized centuries-old cultural sites in the park while learning about the rights of indigenous peoples whose ancestors have lived in the Grand Canyon for thousands of years. This semester, students enrolled in the latest GCS examined and charted water's economic, political, artistic, ecological, social, and spiritual forces in both the classroom and the field, focusing specifically on the Greater Grand Canyon Region ("Grand Canyon Semester").

An integral part of our curriculum for the semester was to use Place as Text, a method of learning created by Bernice Braid (Braid and Long). This method generates active learning in which the student, not the faculty member, is the primary agent; it also employs an expanded idea of "text," the material that is the focus of study and analysis. Active learning emphasizes the idea of charting or "mapping" experiences. Place as Text principles, argues William Daniel, must include an integrated, collaborative learning approach as well as "the complementary values of autonomy and community that determine the ultimate success of the educational process itself, regardless of any specific content or methodology" (12).

GCS courses reflected this method of integrated and collaborative learning, with faculty drawn from different disciplines across the curriculum. As a GCS faculty member, I taught a humanities and aesthetics course called *Writing the Canyon*. The curriculum offered samplings from Greater Grand Canyon-specific art, literature, poetry, and music. Students were required to write and reflect on their own observations using course material that they read or a piece of art they had considered. They drew from their experiences, in both the field and classroom, over the course of the semester and integrated their reflections through in-class discussions, personal journaling, online responses, peer-review writing workshops, and short essays. Instead of a traditionally formal end-of-semester paper assignment, I asked students to create a "cultural map" of sorts with accompanying interpretation. This assignment gave students a chance to chart, in their own ways, complex experiences they captured through observation and reflection throughout the semester and make sense of them in a unique manner.

Cultural mapping is not a complicated idea. Every day people use maps of all kinds to define their world. Maps can be powerful tools that tell us what places and experiences are important to a particular culture; maps can also intentionally misrepresent the importance of place to a particular group if that place is omitted from a map, thus weakening the spiritual or emotional significance of a place to the culture, according to Jim Enote, a Zuni Indian and director of the A:shiwi A:wan Museum and Heritage Center in New Mexico (ctd. in Enote and McClarran 189–92). Enote was inspired to create his Zuni Mapping Project, a series of different paintings that, under Enote's direction, Zuni artists have crafted to represent the many culturally sacred places in their own world. Using Enote's cultural mapping idea, I drafted an assignment that asked students to create their own end-of-semester cultural map, combining their unique perspectives and experiences in a creative and personal manner that told their own story.

We began the assignment with a general discussion of maps: what they do, what they do not do, and how and why maps might oppress as well as empower a group. Foundation readings on cultural mapping followed, and throughout each class I continued to ask students to consider how the course samplings mapped a particular aspect of the Grand Canyon region as well as the unique stories of the authors.

I also included a collaborative in-class cultural mapping exercise that asked students to first individually draft a map of the Greater Grand Canyon region and then add to it geological, geographical, and cultural resources that they deemed important to their semester's experience. They could make these map notations bigger or smaller, colorful or not, depending on their importance.

They could, but did not have to, label the notations or use the colored pencils, paper, watercolors, and markers I provided for them. This exercise was simply an entry point to introduce the idea that maps can tell profound stories of others as well as themselves. They were also asked, as they made these initial maps, to informally capture the following on paper:

- why the particular elements of their own map were important;

- what their favorite form of "writing" was (poetry/short stories, essays, journals, painting/sketching, sculpture, songs, videos, or other multi-media projects); and

- how they might translate their findings into a mapping project that reflected their Grand Canyon Semester experience.

We followed with a class discussion, comparing our choices and talking about what surprised students and what did not in our comparisons: why one student included this particular place or experience, for example, while another student chose to leave it out. The goal of this exercise was to remind them to consider their own stories and the lessons they had learned during the GCS and to provide a way for them to take these lessons back to their home colleges to share. Next, we integrated these experiences into something tangible they could reflect on and take home when the semester ended. Last, we displayed some of the finished products in a studio setting during our First Friday Art Walk Celebration in downtown Flagstaff, an evening gathering that closed out the Grand Canyon Semester.

On that last night, the final maps highlighted our students' creativity and allowed them to share what they had learned with a larger audience. For example, several students painted "ammo cans"—waterproof metal boxes used on river rafting trips—having been introduced to this equipment during our Colorado River rafting trip mid-semester. Those who chose to paint cans included places and symbols meaningful to them from the Greater Grand Canyon region. Some students wallpapered the interior of their box with significant scenes and symbols while others placed in their boxes meaningful found objects they had collected on field trips. One student created a book with a series of individual pen-and-ink sketches detailing a favorite place; the sketches could be flipped up from their mountings, revealing a short handwritten description about the place and why the artist chose to include it. Still another student filled a small, handmade paper cylinder with rolled lines of poetry chosen from her personal journal and kept throughout the semester. One student created a Grand Canyon board game, complete with playing board and rules. Finally, one student read an essay that made a "map" of his experience via the written word, and two students collaborated on writing and performing a song that not only captured their own GCS experience but seemed to embody, collectively, the group experience as well.

Along with the completed creative piece, the students were required to submit a formal essay that interpreted their project for others. The essay prompt asked them to explain why they chose their particular method of delivery for their map project, to explain their map's particular characteristics, and to relate these characteristics to their semester's learning experiences: what was important to them and why, what was left out and why, and how their cultural map would remind them of their own semester story found within their reflections and observations.

This cultural mapping assignment, brand new to me and to my students, was a resounding success. It allowed students a hands-on way to collaborate with each other and share their collaboration with a larger community via an art show. It allowed students, using their unique gifts and perspectives, to reflect on and capture their personal honors experience. The assignment supported, in a creative and student-driven way, the methodology of Place as Text, which emphasizes "mapping" and integrating unique experiences to achieve fresh and lasting learning outcomes. With adjustments, this cultural mapping assignment can be integrated into other place-based curricula offered in honors programs throughout the United States, allowing honors students a nontraditional way to create and reflect on a physical representation of what they learned over the course of a semester.

REFERENCES

Braid, Bernice, and Ada Long, eds. *Place As Text: Approaches to Active Learning.* Lincoln: National Collegiate Honors Council, 2010. NCHC Monograph Series. Print.

Daniel, William. "Honors Semesters: An Anatomy of Active Learning." *Place as Text: Approaches to Active Learning.* Ed. Bernice Braid and Ada Long. 2nd ed. Lincoln: National Collegiate Honors Council, 2010. 11–17. NCHC Monograph Series. Print.

Enote, Jim, and Jennifer McClarran. *A:shiwi A:wan Ulohnanne—The Zuni World.* 1st ed. A:shiwi A:wan Museum and Heritage Center, 2011. Print.

"Grand Canyon Semester." University Honors Program. *Northern Arizona University.* Web. 28 Dec 2012. <https://nau.edu/honors/gcs>.

Sass, Bert. "Grand Canyon Semester: Learning in the World's Most Incredible Classroom." *12 News Today.* 16 Nov. 2007. Web. 28 Dec. 2012. <http://www.azcentral.com/12news/news/articles/1118canyonwebbonus-CR.html>.

CHAPTER 7

Adapting City as Text™ and Adopting Reflective Writing in Switzerland

MICHAELA RUPPERT SMITH

[Editor's note: What follows is a revised version of an essay titled "Self as Text: Adaptations of Honors Practice in Switzerland" originally published in Honors in Practice *7 (2011): 175–80.]*

City as Text™, the experiential-learning program developed by Bernice Braid and the NCHC Honors Semesters Committee, has been adopted and adapted by hundreds if not thousands of educational institutions throughout the United States and beyond. Having served on the Honors Semesters Committee, I exported this learning strategy to Switzerland while teaching in an International Baccalaureate Program in Geneva. I adapted City as Text for multi-disciplinary college preparatory students in Europe, and that adaptation might now serve in turn as a model for experiential learning in honors programs and colleges in the United States and internationally. The focus and link between the City as Text experiences on two different continents and at two different levels of education will be what I call "Self as Text."

The active-learning experience that is the extension of and variation on NCHC's City as Text involved an educational trip from Geneva to Zurich taken by eighty-five International Baccalaureate Theory of Knowledge students accompanied by eight multi-disciplinary teachers. The Theory of Knowledge course encourages eleventh- and twelfth-grade students, through an interdisciplinary inquiry into "what it means to know," to gain both a summative and forward-looking perspective on their education and on themselves as knowers. The course is most effectively taught by means of active learning, exploring essential questions that challenge students to discover and analyze the major ways in which people know and to make interconnections between these modes of knowing and the subject areas they have been studying.

The trip served the purpose of initiating the eleventh-graders into the course. The students had been told that they would be going to two exhibits. The first was Gunther von Hagens' *Body Worlds*, an exhibit of artfully displayed plasticized human cadavers, skinned to reveal (as the exhibit brochure announced) their "interior faces" of skeleton, muscles, nerves, and organs. The second was *Buddha's Paradise* at the Rietberg Museum in Zurich, displaying two-thousand-year-old Buddhist art. The students also knew that most of the group would be eating dinner at a restaurant in Zurich where patrons eat in the dark. Finally, the students knew that they would be required to produce a criteria-based, graded, reflective essay on the trip activities.

The students, generally between sixteen and seventeen years old, were a multi-lingual and multi-cultural group, and for the most part they were used to that context. All spoke English but in many cases not as their mother tongue and generally in addition to several other languages. As IB students, they were an academically select group. The challenge for the teachers planning the trip curriculum was to determine what kinds of tasks would engage students already well-versed in diversity and difference. What kinds of activities would challenge them to step even further outside of themselves and gain a yet wider perspective on self/other/world? Martha Nussbaum has expressed this challenge eloquently in her concept of "narrative imagination" or "the invitation to become, to a certain extent, philosophical exiles from our own ways of life, seeing them from the vantage point of the outsiders and asking the questions an outsider is likely to ask about their meaning and function" (qtd. in Gillison 34). I see this questioning of self, what I call "Self as Text," as also the end goal of the mapping done in NCHC's City as Text.

In planning the trip curriculum, we were fortunate to have a large choice of exhibits in Zurich to select from, including both *Body Worlds* and *Buddha's Paradise*, but as a creative and motivated team of teachers, we would also like to take some credit for choosing to juxtapose these two exhibits. As is the case in many team initiatives to develop a curriculum, a blending of ideas and possibilities took place among us, a creative and seemingly magical process that was not random but intensely purposeful work. As soon as we learned of these two exhibits, we saw the potential the combination held. How many of our students, we asked ourselves, had already been to any of the controversial *Body Worlds* exhibits? None, as it turned out. How many were familiar with Buddhism in the context of Gandhara, Pakistan, and Bamiyan, Afghanistan, two thousand years ago? Several knew that giant Buddha statues had been destroyed by the Taliban, a fact that was also a central component of the exhibition; however, learning about the earlier historical context of these sculptures and engaging with issues of who decides whether to destroy or preserve the past, and according to what criteria, were something new. Newer still was the process of comparing and contrasting this exhibit with that of *Body Worlds* and issues it raised about the preservation and/or destruction of the human body and, some would say, the soul.

Once we had realized the potential of the exhibits, the rest of the planning soon followed. Since the two exhibits conveyed information first of all through the sense of sight, we imagined a third activity that could not be experienced visually. We decided to take them to a restaurant in Zurich called "Blindekuh," or "Blind Man's

Bluff." The restaurant is completely dark. Patrons enter, are led to their table, and are served a three-course meal in total darkness. We chose not to reveal to the students in advance that the waiters and waitresses were all blind. We were sure that the "Blindekuh" would require some intense and unfamiliar mapping on the part of the students.

In subsequent reflections on the experience of both the trip and its planning, I have repeatedly come back to the process of mapping. In the NCHC monograph *Place as Text: Approaches to Active Learning*, Bernice Braid addresses the crucial role of mapping, by now a core concept of honors teaching and learning. Students and teachers engaged in a City as Text assignment, she says, are asked to observe a place and its people in their given context—what Braid calls "focused observation" (16). She says that the questions are: "Whom do I watch? Why? What do I expect? Why? Am I ever surprised? By what?" (15). Braid stresses the importance of knowing how I, the observer, respond. In the end, mapping becomes a metaphor for a personal voyage of discovery, of learning how to stand on foreign ground and find a new touchstone, a new perspective from which to see. True learning brings forth a paradigm shift in our own journeys of discovery—a new way of seeing that is a new way of thinking and of being within ourselves, with others, and in the world. This magic worked itself out through our mapping and planning of the trip to Zurich as well as the transformations the trip brought forth in our students, who, like their college counterparts, learned how to ask new questions, re-learned how to be surprised by the unexpected, and responded with their own magic mirror of "Self as Text."

As background information for their voyage of discovery, we had provided students with a handout to orient them to the two exhibits and the restaurant. The handout began with the introduction to the *Buddha's Paradise* exhibit from the webpage, followed by a list of orienting yet largely open-ended questions and a page of key ideas or "unifying themes" about Buddhism. We also provided a set of questions to use for reflection on the Buddha exhibit, focusing on the ethics of destruction or preservation of the past.

After having seen *Buddha's Paradise* and looked into her magic mirror of "Self as Text," my student Ethar Abd Al-Shakour wrote:

> The past should be left for the future generations to look back to and reflect. . . . As for me, I wouldn't want to destroy any part of me for the future me because everything I have and am is what makes me *me* and what makes me unique and different from everyone else.

Al-Shakour's words demonstrate the active, engaged learning that went on for this sixteen-year-old student. She reflected on the impact of the contemporary destruction of an over two-thousand-year-old tradition and made a personal connection between the ethics of preserving or destroying the past and the value of sustaining her own identity; this is important learning at any age.

Another student, Rebecca, always a strong defender of her faith, reflected: "I learned a lot about the religion itself, as well, and what I learned from it is not to agree or disagree, but to understand and accept different beliefs." This was no trivial statement from a young woman who was empowered through her active-learning experience to lead others not only from the perspective of her traditional faith but also from a perspective of tolerance that is vital to twenty-first-century global citizenship.

Second on our background handout was a copy of the *Body Worlds* exhibit's mission statement, followed by a page I had put together called "An Assembly of Random Thoughts," which could or could not apply to this exhibit. These thoughts included: "Is it art? Is it science? Is it awesome? Is it disturbing? 'The Devil made me do it,' said Faust. Cultural perspectives on THE DEAD—are you grateful?" The juxtaposition of these ideas was meant to be jarring and to trigger creative reflection on the part of the students.

Diana Baranga responded: "The extent to which science has driven human knowledge is admirable. . . . However, the exhibition was also disturbing. . . . It is true that we use technology for the progression of humankind, but how far should we be allowed to go?" Her question echoes many like it that have been asked about this controversial exhibit and asked throughout history, often after a horrendous event like the bombing of Hiroshima and Nagasaki. The key to knowledge is learning how to ask the right questions, and Baranga ranks as an outstanding student in the questions she raises. I often feel humbled by her philosophical, ethical, and deeply felt contributions to class discussions. She did not ask her essential question about human knowledge lightly.

The third component of the background handout related to the restaurant, and it was a page of questions leading to reflections on sight and light followed by a nineteenth-century poem by John Godfrey Saxe entitled "The Blind Men and the Elephant." While the ancient story that this poem is based on is well-known, not all of the students had heard this tale that underscores a basic honors education call to consider claims as well as counterclaims, to understand that our knowledge and indeed our truths are interpretive in nature, and to realize that any interpretation is one among many and capable of being changed.

In his reflection on the restaurant experience, Jeremy Dejardin noted:

> In fact, the only people capable of serving the food in pitch black are blind people. . . . I started having images projected into my mind's eye of who and what was there. I think my hearing was the sense that deceived me the most because I was focusing too much on it so that I heard things which weren't real.

Through his experiential learning at the "Blindekuh," Dejardin looked at the reflection in the mirror of self/other/world and no longer found in it the same conventional images. Instead, like many artistic and literary counterparts, he had somehow gone through the magic mirror and come out the other side, where "who and what was there" were "images projected into . . . [his] mind's eye" and he heard things that "weren't real." In this dark yet quite vivid and marvelous world, only the blind could "see." For Dejardin, Self as Text took on mythical properties in the "Blindekuh."

Self as Text achieves such mythical properties in large part through its essential component of reflective writing, whereby

68

otherwise transient impressions take shape and become transformed into something more substantial. While memories of a voyage of discovery may be beautiful or in some other way powerful and can be lasting, they are also subject to the vagaries of memory. The act of reflective writing promotes deeper and more substantive thought. Finding the right words, organizing thoughts, adding associative ideas, thinking critically, evaluating and supporting claims—in short, adapting the reflective, inner dialogue to be read and further reflected upon by others—promotes communal reflection and dialogue; this is what transforms ephemeral experience into an enduring body of thought.

The project of Self as Text requires reading the experiences into which one has projected oneself, and this "read" text then engenders the reflective, recursive, and transformative written text that completes experiential learning. The academic journey of Self as Text is not a tourist venture verbally narrated to friends and subsequently stored in one's memory bank but rather, like a hero journey of world literature, bears the essential component of the homecoming, bringing existentially transformative knowledge of self, others, and the world to share with the community.

Another student reflection on the "Blindekuh" restaurant further illustrate these ideas. About her initial experience of sitting at the table in the darkness, Baranga wrote:

> When I sat down, the very first thing I did was to inspect my surroundings. I felt my chair and, in my mind, due to the material it was made of and its shape, I tried relating it to various chair designs I had seen before. By feeling the chair and making sure that it was stable, I felt much more relieved. The chair, for me, was a focus point. It defined my position in the black emptiness around me. As long as I sat on it, I knew I existed in the black space I was in.

By reflecting on what she had experienced at that moment and finding just the right way to express in writing what was significant about this experience, Baranga achieved a level of critical thought that would not have emerged had she just spoken about it or tucked the experience away in her memories. Without ever having received any information about City as Text exercises or their important element of mapping, Baranga had written a precise example of mapping as "a metaphor for a personal voyage of discovery, of learning how to stand on foreign ground and find a new touchstone, a new perspective from which to see."

I think all who went to the "Blindekuh" during our discovery tour to Zurich would agree that, along with the exhibits, it offered stunning new perspectives. The students and faculty who went on this trip came back with the sense of having learned an incredible amount about themselves, others, and the world. Long past the debriefings in our large group and in our various small classes, the Zurich experiences lived on as a reference point in many different contexts. The bonds that had been formed remained strong as well and continued to work their magic for students and teachers.

As teachers we felt that we had succeeded in what we had set out to do. The students had come through their experiential-learning orientation to the course and its emphasis on critical, reflective, and transformative thinking with flying colors. In the spirit of a City as Text "voyage of discovery" (Braid 14) and of Nussbaum's "narrative imagination" (qtd. in Gillison 34), the students had brought about their own paradigm shifts and found new touchstones of reality, new eyes with which to see themselves and the world. We could indeed call this process "Self as Text," which is a lifelong process that both college honors education and pre-college adaptations of it aim to promote. At all stages of their lives, responsible knowers can never stop seeking new perspectives, new eyes from which to see. Through our adaptation of an NCHC practice, these college preparatory students had successfully gone on a communal and individual voyage of discovery. In their reflective essays they later articulated, recollected, and preserved this particular voyage in their narrative imagination. Through their adventure in experiential learning, they had ventured outside themselves, scrutinized evidence, and considered multiple points of view. In dialogue with the community and through personal reflection, they had questioned their basic values and integrated new ways of thinking and being into their lives.

As their teachers, we felt rewarded for our efforts. We had stimulated and supported our students' intellectual, social, moral, and emotional growth, helping prepare them well for the future journey of higher education, college honors, and continued lifelong learning. All it had taken was work and dedication on the part of a group of teachers who, like our students, were willing to embark on a journey of "Self as Text" and make the most of it. In the spirit of honors teaching and learning at any level, everyone had come home the richer for having left. Together we had forged strong communal bonds, charted exciting new intellectual territory, and set new personal goals. We had deepened our understanding of ourselves, of each other, and of the global culture that calls on us to be capable and effective leaders.

City as Text is innately a tripartite process that encompasses Self as Text, City as Text, and World as Text. In honors practices and their many adaptations, we are empowering future leaders of a new, demanding, socially just, and globally sustainable tomorrow. Part of the magic of "Self as Text" is that the mirror is large and multi-faceted; it invites us to embark on a lifelong journey where all of us can find and re-find, invent and re-invent, ways of learning and seeing and knowing in ever-expanding contexts.

REFERENCES

Braid, Bernice. "Honors Semesters: An Architecture of Active Learning." *Place as Text: Approaches to Active Learning.* Eds. Bernice Braid and Ada Long. Lincoln: National Collegiate Honors Council, 2000. 14–22. NCHC Monograph Series. Print.

Gillison, Linda Rutland. "Community-Building in Honors Education." *Teaching and Learning in Honors.* Eds. Cheryl L. Fuiks and Larry Clark. Lincoln: National Collegiate Honors Council, 2000. 33–43. NCHC Monograph Series. Print.

Saxe, John Godfrey. "The Blind Men and the Elephant." *The Poems of John Godfrey Saxe: Complete in One Volume.* Boston: Ticknor and Fields, 1868. 259. Web. 12 Dec. 2013. <http://books.google.ch>.

CHAPTER 6

Writing as Transformation

Rebekah Stone, Nicholas Magilton, Nancy Nethery,
and Brittney Pietrzak

[Editor's note: We solicited accounts of the role of writing from several alumni and alumnae of the NCHC Honors Semesters, and we received responses from students in four different New York Honors Semesters between 1981 and 2003. The first two narratives—like the chapter "Claiming a Voice through Writing" by John Major, an alumnus of the 1984 New York Honors Semester—demonstrate the common theme that writers come into a sense of identity, value, and personhood when they do their first piece of writing and when others who read what they have written acknowledge them in an essential way. Being heard in discussions does not produce this magic, but being read does. In addition to making the writers feel acknowledged, the process of their writing makes them acknowledge the outside world in a way that they otherwise might not. The other two essays present a counter-perspective, illustrating choices either not to reveal one's identity or to adopt a form of reflection and revelation other than writing.]

REBEKAH STONE:
1984 UNITED NATIONS HONORS SEMESTER

I came to participate in United Nations III in 1984, when I was twenty years old. I came from South Carolina, where I had been born and raised, where I was attending the state university, and from which I had traveled very little. I did not come because I was interested in the United Nations—I barely knew what it was. I came because I wanted to get out of South Carolina and because I wanted to live in New York City. I wanted to start the rest of my life, scrubbed free of the first two decades; I wanted to create myself from scratch.

I was smart—I had a plan: I would get to NYC, lose my accent so no one would be able to tell where I was from, and simultaneously both forget the turmoil into which I had been born and make up for the life I imagined it had kept from me.

Turmoil was standard where I grew up, a small town still in the murderous grip of Jim Crow. Ten years of protests, punishing retaliation, and mass jailings of black citizens led to the day in 1968 when National Guard troops opened fire on unarmed students at historically black South Carolina State College, wounding thirty and killing three. I started school two years later, in the first public school class to be integrated. As happened across the South, two segregated academies opened that same year, and the chasms of distrust, fear, and often hatred widened, deepened, and framed the lives of everybody living there.

As a child, I did not know anything different. I only knew that my every move, my every interaction, every word I spoke and did not speak was to varying degrees defined by my race. At school, I was one of a handful of white kids; at church, I was from a public school family; at home, I was quiet, never finding words to navigate the confusion, the fear, the feelings of love and friendship that were illicit, dangerous, to be held inside as if encoded for a spy.

As I grew up and came to read and know that all the world was not like my town, I wanted out. Way out. Early on, possibly because of the disdain I heard expressed around me for Yankees, I decided that New York City would fix the problems of my history. I began to daydream that I lived there, that I was a famous writer who had lived there so long that people thought I was from there. But these were fantasies; I could not fathom that I would ever really get out. College came and so did a letter offering me a scholarship at the state university. Lacking much imagination or any financial resources, I accepted without even applying elsewhere. I got out of town, but only forty miles away. My expectations were modest; I knew where I was from.

So when the chance came to spend my junior year in New York, I would have been willing to study anything—the United Nations would be fine. School had always been easy for me, with next to no effort, even at university. I did not think twice about being able to breeze through any academic requirements, to handle them swiftly so as to make myself primarily available for transformation by the city.

I arrived there early, as soon as the dorms opened. I had declined my parents' offer to drive me up. I flew for only the third time in my life, the first time to a destination other than Atlanta. I hailed my first cab. I remember riding from Queens to Brooklyn, trying to slow my breath and not look young and country. I remember trying not to cry, not to let the cabdriver see how relieved I was that I had gotten out, that I was here, that finally my life was beginning.

The first two days were great, jumping on trains and running around Greenwich Village with the few other students who could not wait to get there. Most of our group of thirty-eight came just before the program began. That is when the big kink in my plan got exposed.

The first night we were all there, amid introductions and unpacking, I walked into the beginning of a game of Trivial Pursuit. The forming teams asked if I wanted to play. "Sure," I answered, clipping my word to mask the drawl. I was good at Trivial Pursuit.

I quickly discovered, even before the first round ended, that I was not good. Maybe I had been good in South Carolina, or maybe a remedial deck of questions was sold there. What I learned is that my new classmates were smart, smarter than anybody I had ever known, certainly smarter than me. They speed-answered questions I did not even have a context for. They used words I did not know. They fought over nuances that did not make sense to me. They scared me; I did not know how I was going to get by. I dropped off my team and wandered away.

At the orientation on the first day, we were asked to place ourselves on the political spectrum. I had never heard those words used together. Left and right were strictly directional cues for me. We were asked in a politics class to introduce ourselves to the professor by writing a paper about individualism. I thought that meant wearing unfashionable clothes and big earrings. I quickly realized that my best option was to shut up and try to absorb some answers and opinions from the brilliant students around me.

And then I got to City as Text™. I do not remember hearing phrases like experiential learning or recursive writing. I only recall being asked to read about New York—poems and stories—and then go out on adventures of our own. This I could do; in this one class, I felt I had something of my own from which to draw.

It has been many years, and I only now recall one adventure that I turned into a "Critical Incident" and revealed in class. There is a granite outcropping in Central Park, not far from Columbus Circle, that overlooks a playground. I climbed it, perched there, breathed in again that I had escaped South Carolina, and looked in all directions.

It is a cliché to talk about the variety of peoples and cultures and languages in New York, especially through the eyes of a young and dumb visitor who for a lifetime had known two categories into which all people cleanly fit—black and white. So I will leave that alone and try to describe what I felt: that the world was larger than I had imagined, that there might be possibilities for me unconstrained by my social history, that I might have a self and a voice and a story that had not been predefined for me by a mean, provincial, warring place.

I wrote about that moment and those feelings for City as Text. I am sure it came out abstract and melodramatic—it would be years yet before I could see myself and my ways of perceiving with much courage and honesty—but it was the start of my bringing anything of my own to the circles in which I lived. After revising the paper, I was asked to read it in class. I was listened to. I was respected and even admired. Now I had one class in which I did not have to change my accent or use words I did not wholly understand. I gained an identity, artificial largely, but it was a first step. I milked it a little. When I felt insecure in Politics, I claimed to have been distracted by a poem or a street fair because now, after revealing this part of myself, I had a reputation and was still in a mind to hide behind it when I thought I needed to. Still, it was a starting point, an invitation in, a way to let myself dare to believe I could ever belong.

That was then—the immediate effect of an environment in which our personal histories and the wisdom and perspectives therein were not only valued but coaxed forward. In retrospect, I can identify other fruitfulness.

The nature of the honors semesters was that we lived and studied together in a setting that was unfamiliar to most of us; that is, we formed a tighter circle than is often the case among college students. We quickly became each other's home base. We kicked around identities and opinions all the time, but the recursive papers we wrote were a more formal, committed expression of what we were thinking, how we were feeling. As I read aloud my words that had been written, examined, pruned, and clarified, and then listened to the same from my classmates, I could hear premises that I held unconsciously, that I had only inherited. I could hear words and definitions from my own lips and questioned whether they matched what I knew and believed. I could hold my own language up against what I had seen and known and, in so doing, begin to weed out what was not mine, hold more confidently what was, and think and feel for myself. In short, I was able to begin the long process of hearing and living out my own story, casting off constrictive and ill-fitting narratives, exploding taboos when that was called for, making up words when a new one was needed, engaging the reality of my own life story wherever I found myself.

Also, from this distance, I can see that my lack of respect and regard for my own voice and history was an already established pattern that was only reinforced upon my arrival at UNS III. I had certainly been part of a small minority as a white student in my primary education, but I was also a child of the oppressor class, skin-toned the same as the crushing power structure, as the fingers that had pulled the triggers in the all-too-recent massacre that became nearly taboo to mention. Putting these identities side by side, I came early to believe that I was not only isolated but guilty. As a means of childish self-protection in this hard circumstance, I had looked outside myself to see who to be, what to think and feel and express, a posture that led to cumulative discrediting and finally loss of my own voice.

I easily resumed this posture in New York when I became aware of the academic deficit I bore as well as the history I felt to be shameful. I discredited what I did know and what I had experienced, putting it up against the gaping holes in my educational background. I tried to hide my history, believing it would only ever be a penalty.

Likewise, as I denied and was frightened by my own story, so too did I become defensive and reactive against anyone else's history and perspective that brought too much challenge to the provincial way of thinking in which I was raised. Increasingly, as that semester and then subsequent years of my life went on, I stretched out this understanding of provincialism beyond South Carolina to include US- and Euro-centric history, political and economic orthodoxy, religion, and patriarchy.

I write all this to say that, had the United Nations Semester been limited to the study of politics, history, and economics, I could more easily have stayed in the stagnancy of thinking with which I arrived. Instead, I was asked to participate, to learn about a place and then put myself there, to reflect on myself in that place, to let my seeing and understanding grow in directions I could not have imagined on that nervous, tearful cab ride from LaGuardia. Then, as an essential step, I was asked to bring this changing view to a circle of my peers, to take responsibility for the words that came out of my mouth and pen, to stand up as myself and take a position, even if it was one that would be challenged by the next critical incident, my own or someone else's. I was asked, thankfully, to speak up, to be a part of a conversation, to belong to a community of explorers, and to welcome others as they welcomed me.

It has been a long time since City as Text, and thanks to many subsequent critical incidents, I may resemble only in height and hair color (and a returned accent once I stopped holding my facial muscles so tight) the girl who rode a plane from Columbia to New York, thinking she could tear up her return ticket and never look back. I have stayed friends with a handful of people from my semester, with two in particular, and we never talk without acknowledging how significant a turning point in our lives that time was. I realize that for me, in a way wholly different from what I intended, it was the start of a getting out, but a getting out by going in. The trap was not South Carolina; the trap was the fear and shame and sadness I carried with me because of what I had experienced in my home state and then tried to hide. The going-in adventure is an ongoing one, but it received a good, early kick-start when I was asked to write about what I saw, felt, drew toward, and fled from in a big new city and because I dared to reveal those ideas beyond my timid notebook and dared to believe I had something to say.

NICHOLAS MAGILTON:
2003 NEW YORK HONORS SEMESTER

I did not know it when I selected my major at Iowa State University (ISU), but I was placing myself forever in an experiential educational and career setting. During my undergraduate career I had the opportunity to participate in three different intensive experiential settings. From a semester-long trip traversing the center of the United States to an experience in the largest city in Italy and finally to a semester living in the economic capital of the United States, these experiences forever altered and determined my course.

Up until my sophomore year in college, I spent my life in places that had fewer than 50,000 residents. A noteworthy experience was traveling to a shopping mall in the capital city, Des Moines; it was the mall after all where people could come close to simulating a cosmopolitan experience because it was the only place where large groups of people met together. Those experiences, however, would not be what eventually led me to desire to live, work, and play in a large city; instead, the three separate semesters I had away from my home university would forever change my life.

My journey into experiential learning began on the ISU campus, where I started to prepare for my career in landscape architecture and to rely on site-based experience for my research projects. It is one thing to look at topography as interpreted by a land surveyor and quite another to travel to the site and walk through it; only then can one comprehend the lay of the land. I first learned this lesson on a cold fall day when our landscape professor sent the students out in groups to map various courtyards on campus so that we could begin to develop our own mapping tools, a primary objective (as I learned later) of the City as Text™ pedagogy. In this case, the tool was a sketchpad, one of the items on the required list of studio supplies.

I knew that, if I was admitted to the professional program in landscape architecture at ISU, I would be required to spend a semester traveling from Canada to Mexico and throughout the states in-between. At the time of my admission into the program, I had not yet realized that I was going to engage in a further experiential-learning environment. Instead, I thought we were going to be tourists visiting the latest and greatest projects involving landscape architecture.

My perspective changed while we were sitting in a room and one of our professors was challenging the environmental policies of a company we were visiting. The owner generously donated (and still donates) to the landscape architecture program. For the first time, I was experiencing someone challenge authority and address upfront the business practices of a powerful company. My upbringing had taught me that such disagreements should not be openly expressed.

I recorded this conversation and other experiences in a journal that all students were required to keep. Although sketchbooks are the common practice in landscape architecture, our professors required that we each write a journal; this was where I recorded my experience of September 11, 2001, my feelings about the trip, my doubts about its value, and my concerns about the profession as a whole. From my drawings I was and still am able to recall things I saw, but only through my writing can I feel as though I am right back in the midst of the experience.

An occasion that required daily journal entries recordings did not occur again until I left North America for the first time. In Rome I was immersed in a wash of sights, sounds, smells, and tastes. I may have been a tourist there the first few days, but, given my exhaustive class schedule and my work on a studio project in a neighborhood off the beaten path, I saw myself as a native. By the end of my study in Rome, I felt both transplanted and enriched. From the early-morning smells and cool temperatures of the Pantheon to the extreme humidity of the sweaty afternoons to the sounds of ambulances that kept me awake every night, I felt at one with the city

I captured my experience of Rome through sketches for class as well as pictures through my camera lens. I had seen these sorts of places in textbooks before, but what a difference it made to be there eating the food, feeling the spray of a fountain on a hot day, and seeing people get cranky from the constant heat. Although I did not make formal journal recordings of all these experiences, writing various notes of experiences down in my sketchbook made me more aware at the time of the complex connections and affections I developed for the city's neighborhoods.

After flying home from Rome and spending several weeks in Iowa, I took off again for the 2003 New York Honors Semester on Building and Rebuilding the City. When I landed at LaGuardia Airport, I was armed with both a sketchbook and an empty journal. I soon hit the streets with my new classmates as we were sent out in small groups to neighborhoods deeper into Brooklyn than we would ever see as tourists. We had experiences in these neighborhoods that we might have read about in travel guides, but we got to see them alive and vibrant, creating our own records in our notes and writings.

Experiences similar to those in Rome were playing out in New York City. I was tasting new foods for the first time and seeing works of art that I had only experienced in textbooks. On one trip to Battery Park City, I recorded the tale of the "snake man" offering those in my group the chance to hold and wrap a giant snake around their torsos, only later to request a payment for the experience. At City Hall Park I witnessed a giant American flag knitted together by a proud woman who had also stitched the lyrics to her favorite patriotic song into her canvas. Once, when searching for an observation to record in my journal, I noticed that the "can men & women," who make their living by recycling, often treat one another—the competition—with greater kindness than the suit types who make millions. On another day while searching for a topic, I noticed that when the rain came, the differences of race and class seemed to melt away and disappear under a sea of umbrellas in which all the people in the city became one mass trying to stay warm and dry.

I was experiencing the city as I imagined only a New Yorker could experience it. Without the exercise of recording these events in a log, however, I do not think I would have noticed or experienced as much of the environment around me as I did: I would have missed so much.

In my current position as a landscape architect, I rely on recording each site visit through drawings or notes so that I can experience and interpret the visit while I design improvements. This essential function results in a better design and an accurate assessment of what is necessary for the construction process to be completed on time and within budget. Unfortunately, as I experience New York City today, I have let my writing and recording exercises lapse and know that I am missing out on experiencing my environment as I did back in 2003.

As a landscape architect and planner, I know the importance of actually experiencing a place fully; merely seeing a place on a map or as a drawing on a piece of paper is profoundly limiting. The game changes when people make a written record of the life that is unfolding around them, when they witness the delicate dance connecting the banker heading to work, the can woman filling her cart, and the tourist absentmindedly walking along the sidewalk. These observations provide a window that gives life, meaning, and texture to a place. As a landscape artist, I must write down such observations in order to do my job well, and as a city dweller, I need to record them in order to experience my daily life with fullness and pleasure.

NANCY NETHERY:
1981 UNITED NATIONS HONORS SEMESTER

> No matter where you sit in New York you feel the vibrations of great times and tall deeds, of queer people and events and undertakings.
>
> —E. B. White, *Here Is New York* (1949)

I arrived with my parents at Long Island University's Brooklyn campus on a hot September day. The landscape of the campus was unremittingly manmade—brick, stone, concrete.

We lugged my suitcase and duffle to the fenced area around the campus. Outside the fence, near the opening, was a chalk outline of a body. I would never learn whether a crime or street art had been committed. Like all tourists and settlers in New York, I had arrived in the middle of the narrative, and the beginning would have to be assumed or inferred.

That the narrative was linear could not be assumed. The city's text had a four-hundred-year head start on us, and it gabbled at us nonstop, without clues for what is significant and what simply is. Take the subway lines: the IRT, BMT, and IND—acronyms whose meaning had fallen away well before we arrived—and then the individual taxonomies within each of these groups like the Lexington Avenue line organized in multiples of two. Are all New Yorkers conspiracy theorists engaged in explaining why there is a GG and an RR but no P or PP? Or was it just us?

We walked streets, some still cobbled, in the footsteps of Dutch and British settlers. We visited an Orthodox Jewish neighborhood where families built huts on balconies of their apartments as part of their observation of Sukkot. One night after dinner, the hostess at an Indian restaurant gave us a handful of seeds to chew on instead of a mint.

Our college narratives from home, largely land-grant universities, had more similarities than differences. We were smart kids from small towns. Most of us were interested in politics or economics and were looking for additional classes related to our majors, exposure to the United Nations, and the opportunity to live in New

York City. During the semester, we would add new branches to our narratives through writing and through observing and moving through neighborhoods. New York would reveal to each of us a different slice of itself, a City as Text™.

You are not the kind of guy who would be at a place like this at this time of the morning. But here you are, and you cannot say the terrain is entirely unfamiliar, although the details are fuzzy.

—Jay McInerney, *Bright Lights, Big City* (1984)

There may be ten million stories in the naked city, but the only one I know by heart is my own.

It was 1981, and we had landed in Ed Koch's New York, not Rudy Giuliani's kinder, gentler version. Although we had not heard of it yet, a disease called AIDS had just been diagnosed. We knew of it only metaphorically from a hot song by Soft Cell called "Tainted Love," which was played at all the clubs that fall.

A steno notebook I kept offers a few clues into my daily activities then, from the Diet Coke-ring and scrawled phone number for the UN library on its cover to its contents: part to-do list, part observation, part rolodex. Here are the address and phone number for Amnesty International's national office, notes about Brooklyn Rediscovery, dates for the San Gennaro festival in Little Italy, an address for a Cuban restaurant, and the title of a song by Quarterflash.

In September, I visited the Institute for World Order, where I duly noted the "present situation: vast inequalities in distribution of resources exist, both among and within nations" and a "great potential of worldwide violence" and "little control of ecological balance."

These problems described in notes from almost thirty years ago still remain, but the proposed solutions, with references to the Brandt Commission report and with calls for a more global orientation, greater centralization, and world-order populism, seem like a message in a bottle from a different world entirely. Even the language comparing developed nations ("the North") to undeveloped nations ("the South") reads like a communication from a non-native speaker. A native speaker would understand that both the South and the North are within the U.S. and that mention of "world-order populism" is rank communism, not to be brooked or discussed.

Steps away from the Institute, I read and wrote at the New York Public Library and the Metropolitan Museum. In the library's hushed reading room, I read from Jacques Ellul's *The Technological Society*. From time to time I would get up and stroll around: The book made me feel anxious and hollow inside, as if it were a great wind aimed at blowing away my most firmly held beliefs about progress, about the future, about hope.

My notebook and the writing we did for class provided a frame in which I could observe the city. The act of writing came easily. I was comfortable with pen and typewriter, a veteran of my college newspaper and survivor of many classes that required frequent paper-writing. I had started making money from writing as a junior in high school when I talked the editor of the next town's newspaper into letting me write a story every week for $15. I figured this would be the way I made my living.

I was less comfortable with where City as Text pushed me: revealing the identities I was trying on. As we passed through different neighborhoods in Manhattan and Brooklyn, I met and observed other people who were facets of what I wanted to be. I longed for many dimensions, to be a writer, club girl, art lover, human rights advocate, scholar.

Each identity required a different setting and, to some degree, different costume. My partner-in-crime, Pam, and I outfitted ourselves at thrift stores and at the used-clothing rack of Canal Jeans. We bought our makeup on the cheap at Woolworth's: peachy gloss lipstick was for class, glittery purple for clubbing. Before dusk fell, Pam and I would consult *The Village Voice* and unfold our subway maps to plan outings: Mamoun's Falafel, the Mudd Club, the Staten Island Ferry, the Kiev restaurant. We mapped a tortuous train-to-bus route to a now-forgotten club in Sheepshead Bay in order to watch R.E.M. play for a dozen people. We knew that public transport would not get us home but were betting that we could get a ride home with the band. My after-dark self was as important to me as the self that spent days reading and writing under the bronze lamps at the library, but I wasn't eager to share my demimonde flirtations with our teachers or in the writing that we did for class. I saw that for some of my classmates, writing the City as Text assignments was more of an act of revelation than one of reportage. I saw myself as practicing for a future in journalism, and I was reluctant to reveal much because the pleasure was in the secret. "I am large, I contain multitudes": the verb, after all, is "contain."

City as Text set in motion a series of street-life adventures and immersion in different cultural traditions. Writing about them did not fit with the role of the scholar-self that I was trying on. Economics and political science seemed more rigorous and objective to me than cultural anthropology, so I wanted a topic that would be taken seriously for the oral history assignment for the class. Back in the spring, in a political science class at the University of Georgia, I had learned of the internment of Japanese-American citizens during World War II. I was shocked and, almost as quickly, embarrassed because all of my classmates seemed familiar with it. Six months later, I was still mortified about my ignorance. I had a deep longing to talk to someone who had been interned and to understand what it was like, so I made a tenuous connection from City as Text to interviewing someone who had witnessed the internment firsthand—because surely in New York I could find someone—and called the Japanese-American Association for help in setting up the interview.

I met the gentleman I would interview at the library, and we sat down to talk in an alcove in Astor Hall. Other people passed us on the stairs as he spoke and I took notes. He had been a child in 1942 when his family was forced to relocate from their home in San Francisco. They were taken to a camp in California, where the family was separated by gender and he and his father were housed with other men in stables. As I heard his matter-of-fact description nearly forty years later, I was shaken, finding it hard to reconcile with the country that I lived in and knew.

The United Nations Semester coursework was demanding, and Thanksgiving was signaling the end of the semester. Instead of joining my classmates in the Berkshires for Thanksgiving break, I went to my parents' house in New Jersey. My family had moved from western New York to a town outside Princeton during the summer, and I no longer had a bedroom or a desk at their house. I set my typewriter up on a card table in the family room and wrote papers, once again finding myself in a place that did not fit after having started to find my place in Brooklyn.

You're funny and you don't know why
You're funny and you can't even try
. . . .
You take a walk and you try to understand
—Pylon, "Crazy" (1982)

Back at UGA, the text had shifted while I was away, and I had trouble fitting back into the narrative. The text of Athens, Georgia, it turned out, was less laden with geographic signifiers and more fraught with social connections. There was no chalk body on the sidewalk to remind me of my anonymity, but, as it turned out, I didn't need one. Missing the fall quarter, I had fallen out of sync with my school-year friends. Relationships and friendships had shifted, people had moved to different dorms and apartments, and once again I was without a map or context. January 1982 was extraordinarily cold: I had arranged to rent a house with my dorm roommate from the previous spring, but the pipes burst in our new place, leaking water that then froze on my bedroom floor. While our house was being repaired, I camped out on another friend's couch and tried to reconnect. I had no car, and my head was full of international politics, music, and painting, but I felt smaller and more lonely than I had in the crowd of ten million. In New York, at least two hundred people always wanted to do the same thing that I wanted to do, usually in a venue designed for twenty. At UGA, I was alone. I ignored my advisor's suggestions and heavied up my class load and brooded.

In time, of course, I readjusted. I found my way back to some old friends and made some new ones. My study habits were now highly efficient, so I was able to try out playwriting and reading and writing about Chinese history while still going out to see music at night. Writing continued to be an act of scholarship, and in time part of how I made a living. I knew instinctively during the semester that writing is dangerous for what it can reveal about the narrator, but I had not understood that if the subject of narration felt imperiled, that too could injure the narrator. I learned to be careful, not just in describing my own observations, as I had been in City as Text, but in the words that I picked about others.

In time I learned that even the identity of the scholar-self or the professional was not enough to protect the narrator. My writing was critiqued by time-pressed editors and squished into PowerPoint bullet points. These stories were told in the media or in boardrooms. I learned to be careful, perhaps even mild. I had not realized that the safety of saying one's own words, exactly as thought, ended at the classroom door.

BRITTNEY PIETRZAK:
2001 NEW YORK HONORS SEMESTER

I arrived in New York City on September 3, 2001. I was excited as I met students from across the country who would be my classmates for the semester as well as my friends for many years to come. I was also excited about the courses I would be taking: City as Text™ and Urban Development as well as Digital Photography and other courses in anthropology and sociology.

It was a Wednesday when my new classmates and I gathered our notebooks and bundled up for a day in the crisp New York air. We were to go to Grand Central Station and meet with city planners to learn about the amazing history of the city through the example of the train station. We got on the subway, which we were becoming quite adept at navigating after only one week in the city. As we crossed the bridge from Brooklyn to Manhattan, Meredith grabbed my arm. Staring out the window, she murmured, "Oh my God, look!" I didn't see anything. More and more people began talking, and the noise of voices rose and then fell to silence. Meredith looked at me and said, "The towers are on fire." That was when everything changed, literally. Everyone was suddenly very aware of the same thing, and no one knew what to do.

The aftermath of 9/11 brought a search for meaning that superseded all other searches. More than anything, I wanted to go to Ground Zero to help. The number of volunteers was incredible. I felt helpless. All I had was my camera, but I was angry at people taking pictures of the destruction. I turned my camera away from Ground Zero and focused on what was immediately in front of me. American flags. Everywhere. I compiled my photographs of flags into a book that now sits on my mother's bookshelf. To this day, it is one of my greatest accomplishments in its turning away from the catastrophic destruction of one symbol of America—the World Trade Center—and its presentation of multiple adjacent images of an enduring symbol: the America flag.

Ultimately, the days following 9/11 shaped the lives of all of us that semester. Many of my classmates moved back to New York to become teachers or artists. Others went on to become city planners, urban historians, or national and world travelers. Thanks to Facebook, we all still keep in touch. I ended up changing my major to anthropology because I liked my New York courses so much. Not only the content of my courses but also my professors and classmates influenced my career path and, more generally, the way I see my life and the world. Now I can read each new place I go as if it were a text, learning from the experiences and creating new chapters in my life. I am never without a camera because I love the act of documenting. I have produced one short film and am working on two more that are nearing completion. Trying to equip myself with the skills to be a responder to national and global health issues such as those caused on 9/11, I am working on my master's degree in public health and completing a bachelor's in nursing.

I realize that my experience of New York was different from that of my New York classmates, who were more clearly focused on the writing assignments that were the backbone of the Honors Semester, and certainly different from the experiences of students back home who did not witness the effects of 9/11. Perhaps because my camera provided the detachment and stability I needed at a time of crisis, photography served me in the way that reflective writing served other students in my Honors Semester. I like to think of it as "reflective photography." Like the writing my classmates and I were doing, taking pictures was for me a recursive form of expression, analysis, and growing awareness of the lenses through which I see the world and myself—the lens of my camera and also the lens of my identity and background.

CHAPTER 9

Experiential Learning, Reflective Writing, and Civic Dialogue:
Keeping Democracy on its Feet

GLADYS PALMA DE SCHRYNEMAKERS

> [T]o provoke our students to break through the limits of the conventional and the taken for granted, we ourselves have to experience breaks with what has been established in our own lives; we have to keep arousing ourselves to begin again.
>
> —Maxine Greene, *Releasing the Imagination: Essays on Education, the Arts, and Social Change*

Maxine Greene's insight into the relationship between learners and teachers and their connection to an ever-changing dialectic is central to the scholarship presented in *Writing on Your Feet*, which is grounded in thinking and writing about situated learning: the teacher creates the framework for learning, and students shape that shell through the lenses of their own experiences and understandings. In the end, both teachers and students "begin again" (Greene, *Releasing* 109). By creating a new paradigm of reflective dialectic through which students can transcend their classroom experience and even their college careers, the stakeholders construct a learning community that prepares students to be engaged members of society. The integration of experiential and reflective learning creates a framework for knowing and understanding the world that is essential for the health of a democratic society. Paulo Freire writes in *Pedagogy of the Oppressed* that "the educator with a democratic vision or posture cannot avoid in his teaching praxis insisting on critical capacity, and autonomy of the learner" (33). The process Freire describes is the underpinning for City as Text™, through which educators have come to recognize that the reflection of experience in oral and written discourse prepares individuals to understand and articulate their experiences no matter what the experiences may be.

Like Freire, John Dewey recognized in 1916 that experience, reflection, and discourse are critical for the health and future of democracy: "A democracy is more than a form of government; it is primarily a mode of associated living, of conjoint communicated experience" (87). Higher education should help students to understand what is needed and what must be accomplished to live in such a society. No matter the discipline or career students choose, colleges and universities are obliged to promulgate the democratic ideal and create an environment that allows for experiential learning along with ample opportunities to think about the meaning of these experiences in relation to their understanding of the world and the individual's place in it. The focus, in Dewey's words, on "associated living" and "communicated experience," on critical capacity, is not new to the American educational landscape, but, given the widely acknowledged crisis in American higher education today, this perspective needs to be enlivened through experiential learning, where a dominant focus is civic awareness and engagement (87).

Reflective learning takes place within a conceptual and practical framework that informs every part of the process necessary to facilitate student growth, particularly as it relates to self-development and participation in a representative society. A 2012 publication by AAC&U's National Task Force on Civic Learning and Democratic Engagement, *A Crucible Moment: College Learning & Democracy's Future*, suggests ways that colleges and universities can prepare students to meet the challenges of this new century: "Today's education for democracy needs to be informed by deep engagement with the values of liberty, equality, individual worth, open mindedness, and the willingness to collaborate with people of differing views and backgrounds toward common solutions for public good" (10). The civic engagement called for can be reached if students are encouraged to become active learners and are immersed in an environment where they reflect on their experiences and analyze who they have become as a result of understanding the lives they live.

This framework for learning beyond the limits of traditional pedagogy invites both students and faculty to think of new ways to achieve social value and self-satisfaction through learning opportunities that broaden the experiences of liberal education. In her chapter on "The Role of Background Readings and Experts," Ada Long describes the importance of selecting texts that do not dictate any given perspective to students but instead provide a path for reflectivity so that the learner can examine or create connections between the text and the experience:

> The absence of authoritative texts or experts before learners set about discovering on their own is of a piece with the absence of authorities generally in that process of discovery. Just as the hardest lesson for facilitators to *get*, unless they have first experienced this kind of learning, is the role of staying on the sidelines, so the absence of defining texts is an unnerving deprivation for those of us trained in academia. (24)

Therefore, in selecting reading materials for an experience such as City as Text, the instructor must opt for works that do not just provide factual descriptions of places, events, and cultures but invite faculty and students to see beyond traditional constructs and to think critically about both the individual and the society in the locations being explored. In *Ways of Seeing*, John Berger speaks for texts that help people perceive their surroundings prior to their developing opinions or prejudices about those surroundings:

> It is seeing which establishes our place in the surrounding world; we explain that world with words, but the words can never undo the fact that we are surrounded by it. The relation between what we see and what we know is never settled. Each evening we see the sun set. We know that the earth is turning away from it. Yet the knowledge, the explanation, never quite fits the sight. (7)

Like Long and Berger, Bernice Braid, in her chapter "History and Theory of Recursive Writing in Experiential Education," suggests that "active alternatives to passive learning could be mechanisms for significantly expanding the nature and scope of learning" (3). Furthermore, Braid advocates the relationship between teachers and learners that, in the 1970s, "emerged in discourse about knowledge and discovery that examined critically the culture of the academy" (3). Braid is suggesting a fundamental change in the academic culture as it has been practiced since its inception in the Middle Ages, where students are the audience to a running monologue, where they take in and repeat what they hear in a typical lecture scenario. Howard Gardner, in *Five Minds for the Future*, recalls a conversation with a psychology colleague about her class in China that speaks directly to his sentiments about a large portion of the traditional academy:

> I felt that her college class, a simple recitation by one student after another of the seven laws of human memory, was largely a waste of time. With the aid of an interpreter, we talked for ten minutes about the pros and cons of different pedagogies. In the end my colleague cut off the discussion with these words: 'We have been doing it this way for so long that we know it is right.' (10)

Herein rests the challenge: moving faculty away from a didactic way of teaching and students away from passive learning.

Alice Walker also writes about the importance of hearing multiple perspectives to achieve a richer and more complex understanding of the world; she views everyone as an author contributing to a shared text and writes about this perception in *In Search of Our Mothers' Gardens*: "I believe that the truth about any subject only comes when all sides of the story are put together, and all their different meanings make one new one. Each writer writes the missing parts to the other writer's story. And the whole story is what I am after" (49). Perhaps the college experience should then be more similar to what L. Lee Knefelkamp refers to as the "collective autobiography" of students and faculty, a place where we find our own unique voice and learn to articulate its subtle nuances (10). In keeping with the same theme, Freire, in *Pedagogy of Freedom* (1998), talks about the teacher's role in this life story:

> Nothing of what I experience as a teacher needs to be repeated. However, I hold that my own unity and identity, in regard to others and to the world, constitute my essential and irreparable way of experiencing myself as cultural, historical, and unfinished being in the world, simultaneously conscious of my unfinishedness. (51)

In our era, multiple perspectives are derived not only from conversations, traditional texts, and experiences but also from the new dimension of technology and its all-encompassing effect on the educational landscape. Mark Taylor writes:

> new media and communication technologies have triggered explosive growth in the amount of information to which people have ready access. Not only is the quantity of information growing, its substance is also changing. This has important implications for the reorganization of knowledge and, by extension, higher education. (112)

Coupling inherited pedagogies with traditional modes of learning is no longer effective for students in the twenty-first century when the culture is dominated by extraordinary growth in information and its accessibility. It is understandable that today's students, particularly those who wish to be imaginative and synthetic thinkers, do not conform to the guidelines of the past but instead look to technology as the new means to pursue higher learning.

Given the varied, complex, and competing information from vast numbers of sources, I believe it is now more essential than ever to provide students with ways to make connections between experience and text, whether paper or digital, and one of the strongest, surest ways is to structure experiences and relevant texts in ways that encourage independent and collective reflection about all these sources and how meaning can be derived from them. Through such an enterprise students can find their personal and academic voice. This model of experience paired with reflection is an ideal way for students to manage and understand the multitude of real and virtual experiences they encounter, providing them with ways of perceiving and organizing new information and achieving personal understanding in an ever-changing global landscape. In *Releasing the Imagination*, Greene cogently observes: "I am forever on the way. My identity has to be perceived as multiple, even as I strive towards some coherent notion of what is human and decent [and] . . . amidst this multiplicity, my life project is to achieve an understanding" (24). Greene further asserts the impact of reflective explorations on a free society, saying that in "open contexts where persons attend to one another with interest, regard, and care, there is a place for the appearance of freedom, the achievement of freedom by people in search of themselves," which nicely defines a central goal of City as Text (*Releasing* xi).

If people are to maintain their freedom in an ever-increasing global arena, students must learn the essential tools for understanding and grappling with the challenges of the new world. Tony Wagner, in *The Global Achievement Gap*, characterizes these tools as the "three Cs"—critical thinking, communication, and collaboration—all of which are fundamental to the learning experience of City as Text (42).

City as Text is a powerful laboratory in which participants become sensitive and responsive to the realities and needs of their global society. In this laboratory, students progress through all the steps described by the scholars I have quoted: they connect experience, reflection, and discourse; they use these connections to create a conceptual and practical framework for self-development and social communication; they transcend the passive inheritance of traditional constructs and actively participate in a diverse, global, and increasingly technological discourse; and they develop a personal and academic voice to contribute to that discourse. Progressively, these steps lead toward the freedoms, challenges, and responsibilities of participatory democracy, which depends on individuals who respect a wide array of different voices and have a strong voice of their own to contribute to the conversation.

CAT creates this path toward a strong democracy through a learning environment where faculty and students, facilitators and participants, take themselves and each other seriously, embracing cooperative and reflective ways of understanding themselves and the world in which they live. The pedagogy of the past serves as a resource but not a paradigm for the twenty-first century. The new paradigm needs to require constant experimentation, discovery, and rediscovery, accomplished through the repeated observation and writing that we associate with all laboratories. Educators need to "begin again," to put aside old assumptions and look at themselves and their world with new eyes. They need to achieve the freedom to redefine civic opportunities and responsibilities. City as Text provides a preparation, format, and philosophy for accomplishing this exciting and formidable task.

REFERENCES

Berger, John. *Ways of Seeing*. London: Penguin Group, 2008. Print.

Braid, Bernice. "History and Theory of Recursive Writing in Experiential Education." *Writing on Your Feet: Reflective Practices in City as Text™*. Ed. Ada Long. Lincoln: National Collegiate Honors Council, 2014. 3–12. NCHC Monograph Series. Print.

Dewey, John. *Democracy and Education*. LaVergne, TN: Simon & Brown, 2012.

Freire. Paulo. *Pedagogy of Freedom: Ethics, Democracy, and Civic Courage.* New York: Rowman & Littlefield Publishers. 1998. Print.

—. *Pedagogy of the Oppressed.* 30th Anniversary Edition. New York: Continuum, 2001. Print.

Gardner, Howard. *Five Minds for the Future.* Boston: Harvard Business School P, 2008. Print.

Greene, Maxine. *The Dialect of Freedom.* New York: Teacher's College P, 1988. Print.

—. *Releasing the Imagination: Essays on Education, the Arts, and Social Change.* San Francisco: Jossey-Bass Publishers, 1995. Print.

Knefelkamp, L. Lee. "Seasons of Academic Life: Honoring our Collective Autobiography." *Liberal Education* 76 (May/June 1990): 5–11. Print.

Long, Ada. "The Role of Background Readings and Experts." *Writing on Your Feet: Reflective Practices in City as Text™*. Ed. Ada Long. Lincoln: National Collegiate Honors Council, 2014. 23–32. NCHC Monograph Series. Print.

National Task Force on Civic Learning and Democratic Engagement, and the Association of American Colleges and Universities. *A Crucible Moment: College Learning & Democracy's Future: A National Call to Action.* Washington, D.C.: Association of American Colleges and Universities, 2012. Print.

Taylor, Mark. *Crisis on Campus: A Bold Plan for Reforming our Colleges and Universities.* New York: Knopf, 2010. Print.

Wagner, Tony. *The Global Achievement Gap: Why even our Best Schools Don't Teach the New Survival Skills Our Children Need— and What We Can Do about It.* New York: Basic Books, 2008. Print.

Walker, Alice. *In Search of Our Mothers' Gardens: Womanist Prose.* San Diego: Harcourt, 1983. Print.

CHAPTER 10

The Whole Journey:
Observations, First Impressions, and Turning Point Essays from Faculty Institutes

SARA E. QUAY, ADA LONG, AND JOY OCHS

Faculty Institutes typically explore the relationship between two different sites within close geographical proximity. Writing assignments—First Impressions, Observations, and Turning Point essays—may span the two sites or address them separately, but they generally follow the format described in this monograph. The First Impressions provide an unmonitored set of unreflective reactions that are later invaluable as the writer gains clearer understanding of a new place and thus also awareness of the assumptions and biases that affected the First Impressions. The Observations delve more deeply into the meaning of a place, producing keener insights into its people and dynamics and into one's own reactions. Finally, the Turning Point essay asks the writer to identify and describe the moment or event or revelation that created some change in perspective on both the site and the self. The Turning Point essays are often published in a booklet when all the participants have had a chance to refine and revise their writing after returning home.

Below are three sets of writings produced during NCHC Faculty Institutes. The first set by Sara E. Quay provides full sequences of writing about both sites explored in the Faculty Institute titled "Death and Desire in the American West: Las Vegas/Death Valley." The second set by Ada Long grew out of an Honors Semesters Committee workshop on City as Text™ practices that took place in the Peruvian Amazon, first in the city of Iquitos and then in the jungle. The third set of writings, by Joy Ochs, came from her experience in the Faculty Institute on "Miami and the Everglades: Built and Endangered Environments."

DEATH AND DESIRE IN THE AMERICAN WEST: LAS VEGAS/DEATH VALLEY

Sara E. Quay

First Impressions of Las Vegas

I observed many interesting scenes on my first walkabout, but the one that has stuck in my head is a pretty simple one: people gathered in front of the Bellagio hotel. The hotel has a "lake" in front of it and a kind of promenade that people stroll down. At regular intervals there are half-moon-shaped areas that jut out into the lake where people can lean over a stone rail and watch the water show. When I was there the water show was not on, but people were in the half-moon areas nonetheless. I observed three different clusters of people: a young man, woman, and baby in a stroller; a group of three friends (mixed genders) drinking and laughing; and a couple holding hands and kissing.

This scene illustrated how ordinary people find ways to use public space for private actions. The half-moon areas are completely public, and whatever is done there can be viewed by anyone walking by. Yet—because they are set off from the main promenade—these areas give the illusion that, if you are sitting or standing there, you are in a private as opposed to public space. As a result, people do things in these areas that they would not do on the promenade proper, including sit down, kiss, feed a baby, and gather with a group of friends to laugh and drink. This private use of public space may be necessary in the city of Las Vegas because so much of what happens here is based on making things obvious, explicit, public.

Even in the midst of such extreme public spaces as Las Vegas, people still need moments where they can step outside of the spotlight to do the private things that make them human: rest, love, laugh. And even in such extreme places as Las Vegas, people will create/find/claim space in which private actions are sanctioned—usually in an unarticulated but nonetheless commonly agreed upon

103

way. The small half-moon areas off of the Bellagio promenade are such places.

I was an observer of the use of this space, but if I had been a participant, I believe I would have felt the privacy of the space even more powerfully because once we step into such spaces we tend to "bond" temporarily with others using the space in the same way, creating a little community, while we also experience the sense of privacy that the space has been designated to hold.

Observations about Las Vegas

Las Vegas is a city that registers and reflects human desires: food, sex, love, danger, fame, and fortune. The city exhibits these desires in different ways when they are masked on the Strip and open outside of the Strip heading toward Fremont Street and downtown Las Vegas. Desires that are often thought of as competing—for instance marriage and gratuitous sex—coexist in both areas of Las Vegas, but they do so in significantly different forms.

Outside of the Strip, sex and love stand literally beside one another: the city's famous wedding chapels are directly beside businesses, flyers, and signs advertising peep shows. The chapels are thematic and somewhat tacky—but they all signify the hope for happy-ever-after. At the same time, flyers for "girls, girls, girls" are in newspaper distribution boxes on every block, and on Fremont Street the women on display at the "Gentlemen's Club" appear to be "live" in front of us, taking off their tops. The juxtaposition brings into contrast romantic love (the chapels) and gratuitous sex (the peep shows). Both coexist here in an unapologetic way, as if to acknowledge that both desires can co-exist in the people walking by. Here it feels as if desire is acceptable—even encouraged and normalized—for visitors and locals alike.

On the Strip, however, where the major casinos and hotels are located, love and sex co-exist in more sterilized, socially acceptable ways. The chapel at the Bellagio is more elegant and sophisticated than the chapels outside of the Strip, and the space feels more traditional and "real" than the chapels with their themes. Sex is present, but masked by words that suggest a more socially acceptable, artistic performance. Images of showgirls reveal them in silhouette—still photos or even drawings rather than "real" videos. The women are dressed in "outfits" and presented as performers. There are no boxes with "girls" flyers on the Strip, reflecting the way that this part of Las Vegas tones down desire by heightening it as an art form.

Turning Point Essay about Las Vegas

The turning point in my learning over the past two days occurred when I talked with the woman working behind the counter at Krispy Kreme. After buying my coffee, I told her I was thinking of moving to Las Vegas and asked her what she thought was the best way to find a job. She told me that the best way was to "know someone." I said I didn't know anyone and asked her what I should do. She replied that I could bring my résumé to the job fair being held today and could try that way. But, she reiterated, the best way she thought I could get a job would be to know someone because then, if there was an opening where that person worked, she or he could recommend me to the manager and I could get the job that way.

Personally, this was transformative because I have never asked someone behind the counter at any of my local donut shops a personal question like this, so in some ways I was connecting with a group of people I only interact with as people "serving" me my coffee. This made me think twice about the service workers I "see" (but don't really see) every day in my own life—people who have networks of connections, community, and information that I do not have.

In terms of my understanding of Las Vegas, this interaction was transformative because it was the first time that I felt I caught a genuine glimpse of what it is really like to live here and what it might mean for someone to move here without knowing anyone. How *do* you find a job if you don't know anyone? And how do you get to know people if you have just moved here? At least in the areas we have been exploring, there don't appear to be familiar social sites, e.g., churches, town centers, libraries, and local coffee shops, where newcomers might meet people. It suddenly felt like a daunting task to break into this world as an employee *and* as a person; I had a surge of admiration for the people who do move here on their own and who must gather a certain amount of courage in order to do so.

This transformative moment was all the more powerful because it brought into relief my own role as a tourist. For tourists, who like the new employee are also "newcomers" to the city, "breaking into" Las Vegas is made as smooth and painless as possible. Maps show tourists the great attractions, but they do not show potential employees the best places to land a job. How do you know where to focus your job hunt? The buildings on the Strip (and even on Fremont Street) do not offer any clues—they face the city streets for the benefit of tourists with grand entrances or welcoming parties to usher patrons through the doors. Where are the service entrances to these buildings? How do you know if help is wanted at a given establishment? What door do you go through if you have an interview? Finally, there is a plethora of information available everywhere—from the airport to hotels to restaurants to billboards—about shows, shopping, restaurants, and entertainment available for tourists. Publications like newspapers, however, that have apartment listings or Help Wanted sections are nearly impossible to find; in fact, I do not think I saw a single one. The world of employment is invisible in Las Vegas, and therefore it is mysterious. In this light, the Krispy Kreme employee's comment that the best way to get a job was to "know someone" may in fact be the best advice a newcomer to the city could receive. It was certainly the most transformative piece of information I received in my two days in the city and changed the way I think about myself and my place in this unique culture.

First Impressions of Death Valley

Leaving Las Vegas and driving to Death Valley was moving from a place that saturates you with manmade images to a place that saturates you with natural ones. Both landscapes are "extreme"—one because it is so artificial, the other because it is so starkly natural. The two places exist on a continuum, and the drive gradually shifted my focus. As we left the city limits, the landscape emptied of anything but hills, mountains, some vegetation, and the occasional building, gas station, or fence. By the time we reached the outskirts of Death Valley, it seemed appropriate that we would stop at a ghost town that might just embody the combination of the two: a man-made place emptied of people and akin to a "natural" ruin.

My first view of Death Valley made me catch my breath. As we turned a corner in the road, the entire valley opened up before us, and I looked down on the salt flats and the empty space. In the distance I could see the sand dunes and what appeared to be some buildings, yet the entire area seemed simply and hugely empty. The scene was awe-inspiring but also unsettling. Thoughts of pioneers struggling to cross the land ran through my head as did a flash of fear about what happens if you get sick or your car breaks down in Death Valley. In other words, the natural beauty was something of a relief from the built environment of Las Vegas, but it brought with it its own anxieties.

Observations about Death Valley

Arriving at Stovepipe Well, where we are to stay the next few days, felt comforting—the manmade little enclave felt reassuring in the midst of the vast open space. At the same time, though, I wanted to resist the impulse to stay close to that sense of security and was happy to head out to the sand dunes to see if I could begin to make sense of the text of Death Valley.

Growing up in a beach town that has some of the most beautiful sand dunes in New England, I felt uplifted and immediately at home on the Mesquite Flat Dunes. They were warm and soft and exhilarating to walk over. I ran up and down. I sat. I lay down. All I wanted to do was pay attention to, and absorb, where I was. My senses—which felt either numbed or overloaded in Las Vegas—seemed more finely tuned on the dunes. I made a list of words that came to mind as I sat or lay on the hot sand: silence, wind, bird, heat, sun, breath, water, vast, plants, height, view, air. As I became more familiar and comfortable with where I was, I noticed the way the dunes formed their own natural "trails" and how people's footprints followed them. I smelled the plants and—despite having been repelled by the scent the first time I smelled it—became drawn to it because of its connection to the desert. I lay down in a grove of trees and breathed in the smell. I heard a fly buzz so clearly I could only stop and listen. Two ravens flew by and I heard, maybe for the first time in my life, the distinct sound wings make as they move through the air. Sight, sound, touch, and smell overtook my usually busy thoughts, and I found myself in a calm, mindful space where it felt like enough just to absorb the experience of being on those dunes. Gone was the anxiety of being away from the manmade environment. It felt, instead, very comforting . . . like meditation or prayer.

At the end of my first day in Death Valley, I have added a new pair to my list of contrasts—which seems to be the pattern emerging from my City as Text™ week. The first contrast I focused on was between public and private use of space in Las Vegas. The second contrast was between sex and love, specifically as they are experienced on the Strip and on Fremont Street. The third contrast was between being a tourist and being a transplant—both newcomers to the city of Las Vegas but with very different points of entry. Finally, today's contrast is between the manmade and natural environments of Las Vegas and Death Valley and, beyond that, the contrasting feelings of comfort and anxiety that both environments evoke, for different reasons and at different times.

Turning Point Essay about Death Valley

My transformative moment has been both professional and personal, but the transformation started long before I got to Las Vegas. It started with an email.

At some point this winter, an email for the City as Text Institute arrived in my inbox, and I clicked on it. The image of what I now know is the Mesquite Sand Dunes stared back at me through the computer screen. It looked hot there, and it was cold outside my office, so I looked long and longingly at the photo. I remembered seeing the poster on the easel at the NCHC conference in Washington. In fact I remembered exactly where it was: beside the book stands at the top of the escalator. I looked more closely at the Institute description and the dates. Spring break week. It could work with my schedule, and the chance to be in the west and the warmth seemed like a good choice in the middle of winter. Besides, I was already incorporating some basic elements of City as Text into my honors course. I could learn more and bring what I learned to my classes the next year. These all seemed good reasons to attend, but life had been unusually busy and frenetic for the previous ten months, and my free time had been scarce. I had already envisioned spring break as a chance to take a few days off, catch up on things, and return rested to finish off the semester, plus I had already committed to visit family in Pittsburgh the weekend before I would have to fly to Las Vegas. Rather than having time at home to rest and catch up, if I attended the Institute I would be away from home for more than a week—the opposite of what I had imagined and, I believed, needed.

I clicked back on the image and read the description again. I thought about it. I pulled it up on my home computer. Something about this opportunity was speaking to me. So I applied for the funding and let that be the deciding factor. When I was told that we could cobble it together from three different accounts, I was suddenly elated. For whatever reason I knew I needed to do this. And so I did.

Professionally, I have experienced a transformation in my understanding of reading places as texts. I teach my students to read popular culture as texts and even have them complete a short ethnography, so the basic ideas were familiar to me. In the process of completing this Institute, however, my ideas about how to guide students through the process of reading a place as a text deepened significantly. I am beginning to see how writing other than academic papers can focus the process and how giving students the frame but letting them paint the picture will enrich their learning and my teaching. I see how the process is at least as important as the product and that my job is to send students out to explore and then listen to and engage with them when they return. I understand that there are places in my courses that can be altered to meet these goals more effectively, and I cannot wait to begin to think this through. I also have been invigorated by doing the walkabouts and explorations myself—not just teaching about them but doing them has re-engaged me with the excitement of observing, talking, interviewing, and organizing information. In other words, I will happily report back to my college that the money was more than well-spent, and I know that I have experienced a professional transformation that can be applied on my campus immediately and intentionally. All of this is very good and very transformative. But it is not the end.

Personally, my transformative moment came in the form of a metaphor. While doing an isolation exercise, I finally comprehended that Death Valley was formed by the elements, the natural forces in and around it. Its landscape is vast and extreme and full of contrasts, the result of centuries of influences that have left their mark and created what is today Death Valley. In a flash of connection, I understood that this is true about me as well. I have been shaped and formed by the elements and forces in my life, and the result is who I am today. This seems pretty basic when I write it down. But to see my life as unique and rich—because of elements that were at times harsh and ravaging as well as gentle and gradual—was exactly what I needed to see right now in my life. I realized that in the end the forces that shape what we are—whether Death Valley or me—simply exist. They cannot be erased or wished away. They have left lines on hard rock faces and across the parched land. But they have also left crescent dunes and alluvial fans that grace the terrain. All of this is Death Valley. All of this is me.

This Institute came in my email as an offer that, for some reason, I couldn't resist. So I didn't. And it changed me.

THE PERUVIAN AMAZON:
CITY AND JUNGLE

Ada Long

First Impressions of Iquitos

Probably every place on earth is full of contradictions—Iquitos dramatically so. My group of explorers—Matt, Jesse, and I—began our first City as Text™ outing by climbing down a steep set of stone stairs toward the river, where tourists or any outsiders are almost surely not supposed to go. Gorgeous banana plants—huge and fruit-bearing, growing out of a thick bed of garbage, a trash dump producing lush greenery. Lots of children playing in the trash, games like soccer, smiling and friendly. Adults—some curious, some friendly, some suspicious—many potential smiles held back. Houses that are less than shacks—some just porches to houses that are not there—riding on what is often a flooded river two meters deep, but not right now. You can see the water marks. People taking fried bananas to market. There is a smell in this city that appeals to me—trash, yes, but not nasty—rather sweet. I noticed it coming in from the airport. Very different from the smells of New York or Chicago, and entirely different sounds coming from the constant buzz of motorized rickshaws, like hornets traveling fast, potentially dangerous but fun, like carnival rides. This place is poor, poor, poor—a little like some places in Alabama, like some villages in Turkey. This is a city, but not one—more like a huge, poor village. I would say it makes me sad, and I think maybe it should make me sad, but it also makes me envious. We passed porches and little cafes crowded with smoking, laughing people, children and adults. Children seem loved here. Dogs run free, obviously well fed, humping each other. In among the poor beaten-down houses are some architectural gems, really original structures, often very colorful and well-kept. There may be areas where the rich and poor are segregated, but here they live next door to each other. Meanwhile, we were adopted by two teenage boys back near the river, who were our guides and protectors. They explained things to Matt, who speaks Spanish, and did their best with Jesse and me and guided us through traffic as if we were children. Was it right to give them some money? Who knows? We did, and they took it but might not have been offended if we had not. People seem to know each other in this town despite its size. I think the boys liked being seen with us. It is obviously not a city where tourists usually wander around. We might have been something of a prize.

Observations about Iquitos

Day before yesterday I was organizing efforts to remove every plastic bottle and empty cigarette package from the pristine beaches of St. George Island and dealing with people enraged that the man who sells ice does not have a trash can for people to put the bags in. Today I walked in Belen Village through street after street of ankle-high garbage that people dump from their houses and little shops—garbage containing animal bones, old vegetables, plastic bottles, unidentifiable papers, all soaked in animal and human waste. When the river rises, it will carry all this stuff off the streets and into the Ykaya and from there into the Amazon. As we drifted by canoe through the floating houses, we saw people swimming in the river, washing in it, fishing in it—my dinner last night might well have come from this floating sewer.

And such is the difference between the United States and Peru. Joy and I were co-explorers on this day's City as Text adventure, and as we walked down to the river, I smoked a cigarette and, as always, flicked off the burning end and carried the butt around in my hand for almost 10 minutes until I became conscious of the absurdity of not adding this tiny object to the mountains of soggy trash every-where. I finally took a deep breath and added my butt to what would become the flotsam and jetsam pouring into the Amazon. So much for eco-consciousness.

In the densely populated Belen Village, housing some 50,000 people, we float past discotecas where men are dancing and drink-ing together. Some are dancing in their canoes. Children swimming at the side of our canoe smile and wave. Women sweep the water lilies and other foliage from in front of their houses—as Joy says, "Mowing their lawns."

Yesterday I was all wrong about the young men who showed us around. They are, in fact, "professional" tour guides. Joy and I spent the day with one of them—Carlos—who took us everywhere as our guide and protector—a 19-year-old Chamber of Commerce. He lives in a floating house on the Ykaya, where he took us to meet his wife—a gorgeous young woman "from the jungle"—and his one-month-old son, Carlos Andreos. To get to the house we had to walk across a long stretch of planks spanning the water, slim pieces of sometimes rotting wood no more than 8 inches wide. The chances of my falling in were at least 50%, but I lucked out today. The house was maybe 10' X 15', with two hammocks, a pile of newspapers where Carlos sleeps, and a hot plate with three pots next to it. His wife clearly is used to visitors and smiles sweetly. The child smiles too and looks as content and sweet as any baby I have ever seen. We meet Carlos's mother, who is smitten with Joy's beauty and smiles nicely without teeth. Carlos says his father is mayor of their little part of Belen.

I had to go to the bathroom, so Carlos showed me to what looked like an outdoor shower on St. George Island, with wood planks spaced several inches apart atop the river. I took a whiz, worrying about penis fish, and looked out over the top of the enclosure just in time to see three other City-as-Texters going past in their own canoe, landing not far from Carlos's house. I thought for a minute that maybe they would be taken to see Carlos's wife and child—that these two were part of an act. But, no, that was a wayward cynical thought. There is opportunism here, but not nearly to that extent.

The day was at times glorious and at times nauseating. Here is humanity without its disguises. Bloody turtles being slaughtered for food, chickens carried by the necks through the market. Everything close to the bone, spilling blood. And at one place in the market that Carlos seemed especially proud of, living creatures for sale—small parrots in terrible condition, a tiny monkey and a larger one (can't remember the names of them right now), an owl, two baby caimans. I should perhaps be ashamed of myself, but the suffering of these small creatures makes me miserable in a way that the suffering of humans does not.

Despite all that, I still see this city as a paradise for children and dogs. Dogs are everywhere, and about half of them are pregnant. In Belen Village, which is much poorer than "downtown," the dogs are leaner and mangier, but still for the most part well cared for. Elsewhere, they roam free everywhere but have the look of well-loved house pets. And people here have indoor pets of various kinds that they nurture and love. One lady in a floating house had a little deer of some kind that seemed to play the same role as one of my cats.

Joy is into trying new foods. There was a bucket with large maggots of some kind from palm trees—some crawling around, some roasted. Joy ate some. She's amazing. She and I shared a wonderful roasted fish—palameto, I think it's called—and I tried to forget where it surely came from. Food is of less interest to me, but I got excited by all the stuff to smoke. I bought a bag full of local cigarettes. I gave 5 soles to the beautiful lady who sold them to me (so many of the people here are drop-dead gorgeous, almost all brown-skinned and most looking very healthy and, it seems to me, happy). Five soles was a bit too much, so she threw in seven extra cigarettes "from the jungle"—three of which she said were hallucinogenic.

As I write this, I look across the street and see a man who stands there all day long every day. I cannot imagine what he is doing or thinking.

Further Observations about Iquitos

I spent the morning in a section of Iquitos called Bellavista. On this day my CAT group consisted of a married couple and me. We went on another boat ride, this time down the Nanay to where it joins the Amazon, which is marked by whirling eddies of water. Then we went up the Nanay for a bit, which is, as I had expected, like the Apalachicola River in its foliage, but it is dotted with the now-familiar huts with thatched roofs.

After the river, we walked and walked in the oppressive heat on streets with hovels pretty much all the same. I am absolutely puzzled how anybody makes a living there outside of driving motocars or "guiding" tourists. Every house seems to have a little shop in front that sells orange juice and odd (to me) fruits. Who can possibly be buying this stuff since everybody else is selling the same thing?

I now judge the quality of a place by the condition of its dogs, and the dogs were mostly flea-bitten and miserable beasts. The females have distended and damaged dugs; the males have balls that hang half-way down their back legs. They all desperately need some flea medication. These dogs were much worse than those in Belen, whereas the dogs anywhere near our hotel are handsome, fine creatures, well fed.

I think my infatuation with Iquitos experienced a setback today. Perhaps the heat and humidity are getting to me. Perhaps I am just tired. But I was more intensely aware of not being able to interact in a satisfying way with the people here even though they are all extraordinarily kind and friendly. Unless they are trying to hire on as your guide, they look at us impassively, but if I smile and wave, they are downright exuberant in their response. That feels great. And in a way I am really impressed and envious that people here seem to be content simply to be alive and to sit or walk or swim and just be. That state of being is kind of an aspiration for me, and so totally different from America, but it also makes me uneasy. On my island, I try to achieve that sense of living in the moment, but I am always assessing the state of my garden or my cats or my household, thinking of what needs work. The idea of not centering my life on work is immensely appealing but apparently impossible. Maybe that is why today was not as pleasurable for me as my first two days here—a kind of worry about my own inability to just be.

First Impressions of the Jungle

We all motocarred to Bellavista and then skiffed to the *Nenita*, the Proyecta Amazonas boat that took us down the river. Except for its spectacular expanse, its dark brown color, and the quantity of floating trash for a few miles south of Iquitos, the Amazon is like the Apalachicola River. What was surprising about the Amazon, though, is that there is regular development along its banks, not

American-style development but thatched huts and fields of banana plants and sugarcane. One does not go far without seeing people along the banks, washing clothes or fishing or just watching the boat go by, which seems to provide entertainment. When we waved and smiled, almost everybody waved and smiled back at us. It did not take me long to figure out that on the Amazon and in the mother jungle ("Madre Selva"), as in Iquitos, we were always being watched as we were watching.

It seemed strange to spend the day having a committee meeting, but we were mostly dutiful except for a stopover at a local moonshine depot. The man who runs it, originally German, has a huge, horse-driven, wooden wheel that juices the sugarcane, which is then fermented in a wood trough that looks like a canoe, from which it runs into a metal vat to be cooked, the condensation rising through a tube and funneled into wonderful old bottles. He also makes molasses. We tasted four kinds of the sugarcane/rum he makes and had molasses on crackers in his open-air thatched house; an old German clock hanging on a vertical beam seemed surreal in the jungle.

After about ten hours and just as the sun was setting, our boat turned into a small canal where suddenly we were very close to the lush vegetation and a great variety of birds. The canal led to the Oroza River, and all along it we could see little fires burning in huts as families made dinner at the end of the day. The huts were spaced maybe a half a mile apart, sometimes in little groups or small townships. Before too long, we pulled into the Project Amazonas compound, where a thatched mess hall is closest to the river, then up the hill a thatched classroom building, then further up a concrete building of toilets and showers, above that a thatched hooch with four little wood beds (I slept in one of these), then much further up the hill, five or six tents, and at the top of the hill a four-story tower for watching birds at the top of the jungle canopy.

As we left the mess hall to settle in our quarters after a great dinner, Joy shone her flashlight on a huge tarantula right above my head. When I got up to go to the bathroom in the middle of the night, there was a two-inch-long black scorpion right inside the doorway—I nudged him with my flashlight and he scuttled away. The heat was so oppressive that it was impossible to sleep even though I took off all my clothes and removed the mosquito netting, but at about 1:00am a light rain started and instantly cooled off our hooch, which was a screened-in, wall-less enclosure. Sleep came right away after that.

The next morning after a great breakfast (all the meals were great, so I'll stop saying that), we spent about two and a half hours walking through the woods and looking at vines and trees of all kinds, bats, birds, lizards, streams, fruits, berries, nests. . . . We each ate an ant to taste the slightly tart, citric flavor of formic acid. We walked through the "devil's valley" of the leaf-cutting ants and over rickety log bridges and around huge trees, which remind me of cypress, from which one can cut an oar straight off the tree because of the way the trunks grow.

Observations about the Jungle

"Jungle as Text" has its own observations, micro- and macroscopic, from the tiniest red spider to a tree that seems to reach infinitely upward and out of sight. Reading this text has its own kinds of mapping, where one gradually becomes attuned to the paths, recognizing logs that block the trail or patches of shoe-sucking mud that can tumble you on your butt in an instant. It has its own sounds—from rain on the canopy to bird whistles to unidentifiable scuttlings through dead leaves. And reflection is a state of being rather than a conscious effort.

After lunch, I saw Joy returning from a swim in the Amazon. I hadn't thought I'd be able to risk that, but I did, and it was wonderful. Cool water and, though brown, seeming clear and desirable. I swam out the short distance to the raft and back, not willing to take on the swifter currents as I might have done when I was younger, a few thousand cigarettes ago. And then a troop of us was skiffed upriver to drift back in kayaks on those swift currents. That was one of my four favorite times on the Amazon, being all alone except for the black-necked hawk who flew ahead of my kayak as if she were a tour guide. At first we kayaked on a small tributary called the "shortcut" in Spanish, and then we entered the Oroza, where we had to paddle when we wanted to but really never had to if we were willing to just take our time. When we got back to the Amazonas compound, the Callao Pilsen tasted its very best. I did a good job of downing Iquitena, Cuzcena, and especially the large bottles of Pilsen.

After dinner that night, we went on a night hike in the jungle and saw all manner of toads and frogs and salamanders and spiders and bats. I fell on my butt in the mud—something of a baptism, I suppose, to be dipped in the jungle.

We had a good sleeping night with rain falling on the thatch roof and a delicious cool breeze. Perhaps I have not said much about the heat and humidity, which kept me soaked with sweat much of the day and, worse, at night. But the clouds and the rain were a delight.

The next morning I climbed the tower to watch the birds and all the greenery and just experience the tranquility of being high up where so many of the jungle creatures make their home. I am terrible at remembering the names of birds but quite good at enjoying them nevertheless.

After breakfast, we all climbed into the skiff and motored down to visit a small town called Comandanzia or something like that (I wrote down the name—I'll find it sometime). The village was expecting us, and the largest thatched hut in the village was filled with mostly women and also some men and children selling the crafts they had made. They prefer to barter (or, as Bostonian Susan said, *botter*), but they would also take soles. I bartered my binoculars and flashlight and some hair conditioner and a shirt for two wonderful little dolls, a woven bag, a bag made of shells, and three bowls made of . . . oh dear, another forgotten name. My bowls were decorated with birds and a scorpion. At one point the "presidente" of that federation made a little speech of welcome, exactly like a university president welcoming a visiting conference. It seemed funny to me at the time . . . but not later when I got to know him.

The buying/selling experience was one of those occasions that made me uneasy, kind of like visiting a Native American village in the Southwest where the whole thing seems some awful combination of condescension, colonialism, humiliation even, and yet you know they need the money and are compromising the integrity of their culture out of necessity. I felt like an intruder, an invader, a Pizarro.

At Comandanzia—and everywhere in Peru—there seem to be three or four young children for every adult. The ratio of dogs to adults is about equal. One sees occasional cats, but more chickens.

Turning Point Essay about the Peruvian Amazon

Back at our Amazonas camp, we had a big lunch, of course, and boarded the *Nenita* to go back to Iquitos. Before I say good-bye to Project Amazonas, I have to say something about Devon Graham and the project and also the extraordinary crew at the camp. A few times on the trip, I felt like the ugly American, but Devon is truly the beautiful American. I had no idea before I went on this trip what he has accomplished in the Amazon: I did not know that he really started the project and keeps it going; I did not know how ambitious the project is (not quite the scope of *Fitzcarraldo* but certainly a lot more beneficial); I had no idea that he had managed in this very foreign place to build a real community of mutual trust and respect and cooperation for the benefit of the local people and for the education of hundreds of students who include high-schoolers and research biologists. Devon has managed to create this community with the help of an extraordinary crew. They are always there, always serving, always helping, mostly invisible. On our hikes, Devon was the visible presence with us, but at least two of the crew were always out in the jungle somewhere, and, if they saw something interesting, would give a yell to come see. They came with us everywhere, protecting us, taking care of us, loading our heavy luggage, making us feel comfortable, feeding us magnificently. Their knowledge is profound, and their kindness extraordinary. Although they were working for us, I always felt that they worked for us in the way that I worked for my students. They were not servants; they were colleagues and professionals.

As we motored down the Oroza to join the Amazon, we saw children and mothers and men fishing who waved and smiled at us all along the edges of the river. Suddenly the skiff caught up with us and Manuel, the presidente of Comandanzia, boarded our boat along with his son. Manuel needed to see a doctor in Iquitos and so caught a ride on the *Nenita*. I never learned what his illness was. I spoke with him as best I could, which was very little indeed, but throughout the 24-hour trip back to Iquitos I started to feel very close to him and to his handsome son, Aldo, 17 years old. Manuel looks 70 but may be 45—hard to tell. Manuel and his son slept on the back deck of the boat while we gringos had comfy cabins, and he ate with the crew. Devon was very kind and solicitous toward him, as were the crew, and I suspect he was very grateful for the ride to Iquitos.

I cannot explain what human thing happened between Manuel and me, all nonverbal and based on very little contact of any kind. But somehow all the unease I had felt in Bellavista my last day in Iquitos as well as all the unease I had felt in Manuel's village of Comandanzia became kind of beside the point, or at least so I felt. There was a connection, a respect. His obvious wisdom and stoicism and strong center of being were a testimony to the decency and personal power that humans can achieve—a power I sensed much more vaguely and uncomfortably among the impassive people we encountered on the streets of Bellavista. When we landed in Iquitos and we gringos got off the boat first, I found Manuel to say good-bye. I reached out my hand to shake his, and he gave me a warm hug and as kind a smile as I can imagine, which brought tears to my eyes. That was my second favorite experience in Peru.

My third favorite experience took place earlier in the trip back to Iquitos, and it also moved me to tears. We were motoring through a small channel between the Oroza and the Amazon when some of our company spotted a troop of monkeys high in the trees to our left. I could not see them at first, but then started noticing the motion of tree limbs bending under their weight as they jumped from tree to tree parallel to our boat. There may have been 20 or 30 of them, swinging and jumping great distances in what struck me as the most joyous expression of freedom and fun I can remember. They kept up with the boat as long as they could, and, as they disappeared from sight, I started crying and could not stop, maybe tears of joy, maybe of envy, maybe of love for our little cousins absolutely free in a way that so few of earth's creatures ever can be any more. I cry even now as I write of it, and I do not understand what I am feeling, this sadness and joy mixed together.

A few miles south of Iquitos we spotted another bunch of monkeys up in the trees, who jumped down to the ground and ran out to a dock and beckoned us to come over. Everybody wanted to stop except me; I was afraid it would be a zoolike experience, and I just cannot visit zoos any more. I felt that these animals, like some of the peoples of the Amazon, would be on display for commercial gain or for "cultural preservation," which I admire but which makes me queasy. We all went, though, and it turned out to be my fourth favorite experience. It was a preserve for orphaned or injured or diseased monkeys and birds and anteaters and any other forest creatures. The monkeys were entirely free except for a few who were either ill or aggressive. As I went over to greet a group of them, a mother stuck one of her babies on her back and ran over to me, dumped the baby, and jumped into my arms. Another time two monkeys in a tree over my head played a game of "steal the hat," where one monkey would sweep down and take my hat, and, as I pulled it back from him, the other would land on my shoulder and pull the hat in another direction. All of us had personal encounters with the several species of monkeys who lived there—maybe 50 monkeys in all—who played with us and cuddled and played with each other and showed off for us and for each other and just for themselves. It did not move me as the wild troop of monkeys had, but it made me laugh and have fun.

In retrospect, I think that what struck me most about both Iquitos and the Amazon was the lack of fear. Everybody in America is afraid all the time—afraid somebody will steal their stuff either through burglary and mugging or through Internet theft and financial corruption. People sign contracts about every tiny detail of their lives; they sue and get sued; they trade their freedom and their wisdom for avoidance of risk or liability. They turn their homes into fail-safe fortresses. In Peru, all the houses are wide open to whatever happens to come in, be it human, animal, or insect. I know there is meanness there (like the sale of wild animals in the market), as there is everywhere, and there is plenty of scamming going on, of course, along with considerable opportunism. I loved Matt's notion of a "gringo alert" that seemed to go out immediately and spontaneously throughout Iquitos so that everybody knew there were some new tourists in town that might, like me, be willing to overpay for everything. My favorite example: All the people outside the window of our hotel lobby were selling trinkets and T-shirts (called "polos" there) until they found out we were leaving for the Amazon the next day; they showed up the next morning with ponchos for sale. But nobody ever asked to be paid in advance; people took us into their homes and seemed to trust us entirely. The city was full of dogs, and I never saw a single one that seemed dangerous or unfriendly; the same was true of the people. The jungle seemed the same way. Animals followed us around without fear: the wild monkeys followed along next to our boat as long as they could keep up; a pink dolphin crisscrossed in front of our boat for almost ten minutes; the black-necked hawk followed me in front as I kayaked. I have tried hard to think of either animals or people who seemed afraid of us or of anything, and I cannot. I would not give up the life I have in America, but, oh how much I and all of us have given up to have this life!

MIAMI AND THE EVERGLADES:
BUILT AND ENDANGERED ENVIRONMENTS

Joy Ochs

First Impressions of Miami Beach

What first struck me about Miami Beach was the amount of development—massive high-rise housing buildings were crammed cheek by jowl with sidewalk cafés and hotels—way more development than I was led to expect from the pre-Institute readings. The density of human beings on this relatively narrow strip of land was astounding to me. At 9 o'clock on a Wednesday night, the sidewalks buzzed with diners and pedestrians. On a Wednesday night! I imagined that to be a resident in Miami Beach is to be in a semi-permanent state of festival. The shuttle driver, however, talked about the downside of living here and the danger of hurricanes.

This morning I walked down to the beach by daylight. The white sand, streaming light, and bleached façades of the beachfront buildings reminded me of the Riviera at Cannes. As a study-abroad student in 1990, I was lucky enough to live two weeks with a family in Cannes, and that experience gave me a different insight into what it might be like to live a normal routine in a place like Miami Beach (where "normal" includes going for a morning run on oceanfront beach and walking children to school by navigating a course through the tables at a sidewalk café). Sure enough, I saw several mothers walking their children to the elementary school near our hotel.

I am surprised by how multi-ethnic the population is here. At the airport, the only Caucasian I saw turned out to be a German tourist. Hardly anyone speaks English. Also, coming from Iowa in January, I am dressed completely wrong for how hot and humid it is here. I feel like I have landed in an alien place.

Observation on Flamingo Park Area

The theme of my observations today was the residential aspect of Miami Beach. My group was assigned the Flamingo Park neighborhood. A few blocks west of the beachfront touristy area, this neighborhood seemed to be designed for the people who *live* here. It included Flamingo Park itself (the only significant area of green space reported by any of the groups today although—with my Midwestern sensibilities—I did not find the park remarkable at all until I learned it was apparently the only one). The neighborhood also included moderately well-maintained low-rise apartment/condominium complexes as well as a scattering of single-family dwellings. Homes boasted small fenced lots. Architecturally, the buildings were in the Mediterranean style, with stucco façades and orange tile roofs. Quiet residential streets bordered the park. At the west boundary of this neighborhood, Alton Street formed a commercial district very different from the one closer to the beach. The businesses offered the kinds of amenities that residents, rather than tourists, would need: barber shop, bank, drug store, gas station, pet store, dentist, day care. Insofar as there were restaurants, they were chains (Subway, Dominoes, Papa John's, Einstein's). This suggests that tourists will eat at the expensive, quirky, local joints, but that residents do not need "local flavor" and prefer to eat the bland fare of Americana.

In sharp contrast to the modest Flamingo Park neighborhood, the bayside properties west of Alton Street consist of high-end, high-rise condominiums. The Waverly, which we visited, houses four hundred units, employs a doorman, and sports expensive, out-of-state cars in its lot (including a Mercedes with New York plates that read SoBeNY). Reports from other groups suggested that high-density housing dominates the housing market here, which makes me see the Flamingo Park neighborhood in retrospect as quaint and idyllic. Residents walked their dogs to the Bark Park—a doggie playground within the green space. One resident, Luis, told us he was within walking distance of everything he needs. Several young men were practicing their soccer moves. A German catalog company was doing a low-key photo shoot of young girls in sports clothes against the backdrop of the baseball field. The park served as an island of quiet in an otherwise frenetic city.

The people we encountered in the Flamingo Park neighborhood were either Anglo or Hispanic, in about equal numbers (we saw one African-American mail carrier but did not have a chance to talk to him). Signage in the area was in English and Spanish (and in one case in Haitian Creole). One Anglo woman said she sometimes felt discriminated against because she could not speak Spanish. Luis, originally from Cuba, acknowledged that he usually speaks Spanish, but did not feel there was any tension between Latinos and Anglos.

The most interesting place we saw today was the SoBe Thrifty, the non-profit gift shop for Care Resources, an HIV resource group. A prominent sign in the store announced free HIV testing on alternate Wednesdays; another sign over a bowl near the checkout informed shoppers that "due to a limited supply, customer is entitled to three condoms per day." Curious about what cast-offs would turn up in a Miami Beach thrift shop, we went shopping. Clothing items were generally modest, and the brand names once again reflected Americana: Gap, J. Crew, Land's End. I gather then that the Armani Express near the beach must cater to tourists and not to locals. I found a wet suit for $20 and a pair of silver stiletto-heeled hip boots; otherwise, I found the kind of thrift-store stuff you could find anywhere in America.

Turning Point Essay on Miami Beach

The most important part of the day for me was the regrouping of all the participants after exploring the districts they had been assigned. After hearing reports from the other five groups this afternoon and putting the Flamingo Park neighborhood into the context of greater Miami Beach, the area takes on a new significance for me. I replaced a feeling that this was a "boring" part of town with a feeling that this is a remarkable part of town—remarkable because it is the only area that preserves a residential flavor. Residents can grow bougainvillea in their backyards, park in their own single-car garage, walk to the park, the bank, or the dentist, and view the open sky. I suddenly felt protective of this neighborhood when I learned that high-rise developments are encroaching on other parts of the city. Flamingo Park is not particularly beautiful or charming, but it is laid out like a *neighborhood*, which is a rare bird indeed in Miami Beach.

For a tourist, a place is interesting if it provides a taste of the distinctive, the novel. As a tourist, spending only a day or two with nothing at stake, I might have been content with the beach and the shops along Collins and Washington. For a resident, however, a place is livable if it provides safety, services, and a livelihood. In that sense, with its dearth of grocery stores and parking, its high cost of living, and its long waiting lists for services such as Head Start, not to mention its lack of distinctive neighborhoods and green spaces, Miami Beach ranks low as a place to live. Obviously, the thousands who are flocking to buy the condominiums disagree with me.

Somebody said today that the entire industry of Miami Beach consists of buying and selling property and attracting tourists to spend their money here. Yet I also heard today that recent property buy-ups mean that tourists have fewer and fewer available places to lodge. At some point will the economy of Miami Beach be snuffed out by its own excesses? Will continuing development eradicate every sense of the unique and distinctive? I do not want to come here as a tourist to see the beach blotted out by high-rises. And I certainly would not want to live here in a high-rise without the local flavor of the tourist districts. I thought, as did the rest of us, that Miami Beach was the "built" part of our "Built and Endangered Environments," but now I understand that it is in its own way an "endangered" one. Too much rapid growth can make a city fragile, and Miami Beach is caught in a balancing act between accommodating everyone who wants to come here and preserving the sense of place that draws them here in the first place.

First Impressions of the Everglades

I have been seeing the phrase "City as Text™" pop up in my honors correspondence for a long time, but it never really piqued my interest until I saw that the methodology was going to be put into practice in a natural area. A guided educational tour of the Everglades with other honors faculty? Sign me up!

Other than a strong desire to experience the place, I arrived with no strong preconceptions about the Everglades. Media representations, as in the movie *Adaptation* or the Carl Hiaasen novel *Skinny Dip*, characterize the Everglades as a wild, almost mystical place apart, where marginal characters can carry on weird lives uninhibited, untouched, and even unnoticed by society and its conventions. In these stories, the Everglades takes on a mythical weight, like the Deep Dark Forest or the Heart of Darkness. I understood this to be a literary construct, and I guess my only surprise, if it was a surprise, was that the Everglades is such a purely reasonable ecosystem: not a place apart, but an integrally natural place to be. I fell in love with it at once.

Observations and Reflections on the Everglades

Today we began our explorations by doing the "tourist thing" and getting a "guided tour" of the swamp. I hate guided tours. Facilitator Peter, talking about the use of traditional field trips in classes, referred to them as "point and shuffle." What we are trying to do here is something different: creating a space for students to learn from their own experiences. In this sense, the airboat tour was saved from being a Disneyland ride for me by the chance to jump overboard and get my feet down around the roots of the plants. Up to my knees in cool water, feeling the sharp touch of sedges against my shins, I learned that saw grass incorporates silicates into its structure, just as big bluestem does on the tallgrass prairie. The other amazing thing I learned, my toes squelching in the bottom, is that the clayey marl that constitutes Everglades "soil" is formed as acid from decaying vegetation dissolves the limestone bedrock and produces a mat of fertile muck. I have learned about soil formation in littoral forests—that spongy humus—and in the tallgrass prairie. But the genesis of marl grabbed me because of the direct interaction of organic material with the inorganic stuff of the earth's crust to make a substance that is the elemental base of the whole ecosystem.

Next, we did the "tourist thing" in Shark Valley, only we rented bicycles instead of taking the narrated shuttle ride. The bike ride was fantastic in and of itself, and it triggered some reflections about built and endangered environments. I have not been on a bicycle in seventeen years, but when I was in high school I used to jump on my bike every warm spring afternoon and ride fifteen miles to Kaukauna and back. At that time, it was a bike ride in the country once I passed the "last house in town," a green and white two-story whose yard petered out into cornfield. From Appleton to Kaukauna the air smelled of clover, a sweet, heady smell that made me want to ride for miles. Now, that countryside is gone, replaced with box stores and traffic lights. It is impossible even to ride a bike there at all. My bike got put in storage when I went away to college, and I have not bothered to do anything with it since. I had lost my childhood bike route to the same mania for creating new "built environments" that afflicts Miami Beach. Today, even though the Everglades bike path was artificial, imposed on the natural landscape by human design, when I took my first wobbly strokes out into the Everglades that youthful feeling of flying on sweet air came back to me. Here was a wide open space left to do it in! It was amazing how quickly the tourists and other trappings of civilization dropped behind and the vastness of the wilderness opened up before me. The effect was even more pronounced on the return ride because the manmade observation tower was not always present in my line of view.

One of the dangers of living in a post-modern world is the feeling that this has been seen and done before. I feel as if I have been programmed to respond to supposedly natural landscapes in a prescribed way. If the airboat tour had a touch of Disneyland, the animal viewing threatened to become a Busch Gardens safari. Having seen alligators and ibises in "natural environment zoos," it was hard to grasp sometimes that I was seeing these animals in the wild, at home in their natural habitat. It somehow had the feeling that it had all been staged for human viewing, from the alligators lying by the side of the road to the great blue heron gulping a fish. Even the abundance of animals seemed an absurdity of excess put there for our pleasure. Seeing one outrageously colored purple gallinule was a once-in-a-lifetime experience—five of them just seemed over the top!

I say all of this ironically, of course, because it was breathtaking to watch the wood stork unfold its white wings and to notice the yellow eyeliner painted on the little green heron and to watch the purple gallinule stretch its long legs running comically atop the lily pads. But it was not the flashiness of the birds themselves but my understanding of their place in this endangered ecosystem that struck me the most. And again, it all came back to the humble muck, which even though it contained microorganisms by the millions, did not become absurd by excess. Rather, it continues to impress me with the amazing mechanisms of living systems, carrying on, as they always have, impervious to the Everglades' designation as an "endangered" environment. Indeed, perhaps the Everglades are not so much endangered as they are built, first by the action of natural processes over millennia, but also by the human laws that protect this wetland from development. What little development there is—the carefully plotted trails and visitor centers—is built in such a way as to provide explorers with the illusion of entering a wholly natural place. Unlike in Miami Beach, the building enhances and preserves what is distinctive here.

At the end, I find it much easier to write about the natural environment than the built environment. Several of the groups used the word "sterile" to describe sections of Miami Beach, and my writing about that place also feels "sterile" to me—I could not find a soft edge to engage with and ended up compiling impersonal lists of things I saw or did. But the Everglades worked upon me like organic matter upon limestone: dissolving, carving out openings, creating places for life to gain a toehold. If this writing is productive, it is my marl, a fertile muck joining the bedrock of my experience to the living Everglades and creating a soil where imagination can grow.

ABOUT THE AUTHORS

BERNICE BRAID is Professor Emerita of Comparative Literature, retired Dean of Academic and Instructional Resources, and former Director of the University Honors Program at Long Island University Brooklyn, where she now directs Core Seminar: The Idea of the Human. She has been designing and implementing City as Text™ laboratories for NCHC conferences, Honors Semesters, and Faculty Institutes since 1978 and incorporating them into orientations and integrative seminars on campus since 1976. Her publications include articles on pedagogical practices and qualitative assessment initiatives.

GLADYS PALMA DE SCHRYNEMAKERS, Associate Provost of Long Island University Brooklyn, teaches social sciences in the University Honors Program. Since its inception, she has taught Core Seminar: The Idea of the Human and presented her design for field explorations in which students experience and integrate literary work in a societal context. She publishes frequently on the theory and practice of constructing knowledge and assessment.

ADA LONG is a past president of NCHC, member of the Honors Semesters Committee, and co-editor of the *Journal of the National Collegiate Honors Council* and *Honors in Practice*. She is Professor Emerita of English and was the Founding Director of the University Honors Program (1982–2004) at the University of Alabama at Birmingham.

NICHOLAS MAGILTON is a landscape architect working for the New York City Department of Parks & Recreation and implementing portions of the NYC Green Infrastructure Plan. He has an MS from Hunter College and a BS and BLA from Iowa State University.

JOHN MAJOR, while a student at Ohio State University, was a participant in both the Puerto Rican Honors Semester (1983) and the United Nations Semester III (1984), and he later served as the Resident Director for United Nations Semester IV (1987). His graduate study at Syracuse University focused on the role of storytelling in public opinion. John is the father of three and currently lives in Brooklyn, New York, where he is working on a memoir that uses paintings by Caravaggio as points of departure.

ROBYN S. MARTIN is a lecturer in the honors program at Northern Arizona University, Flagstaff. She teaches courses in outdoor-themed, place-based experiential education; twentieth-century history and pop culture; and sustainability, among others. She received her MA in rhetoric and composition and plans to pursue her PhD in interdisciplinary studies in the future.

NANCY NETHERY received her MA in economics from the University of San Francisco. She works in Internet product management in Atlanta and is a volunteer editor of microfinance loans for kiva.org. A participant in the 1981 UN Semester II, Nancy continues to exercise her passions for performance, music, and city living by volunteering for the dance/performance group gloATL at its home studio in the Goat Farm, located in Atlanta's Westside Arts District.

JOY OCHS is Professor of English and Honors Director at Mount Mercy University. Her first experience with City as Text™ was during the 2006 NCHC Faculty Institute in Miami and the Everglades. Since then, she has embraced the pedagogy and become a facilitator for NCHC Faculty Institutes in the Twin Cities, Kentucky Cave Country, and Yellowstone. Miami is still her favorite.

BRITTNEY PIETRZAK is a research assistant at the University of Alabama at Birmingham School of Public Health. She has worked on multiple research projects for health behavior and quality of life improvement. She continues to document the world around her through photography and writing, while public health research allows her to represent populations through the use of statistics.

SARA E. QUAY is Director of the Endicott Scholars Honors Program at Endicott College. Her research focuses on cultural studies, teaching and learning, and higher education. She has been a participant and facilitator of NCHC Faculty Institutes in Las Vegas/ Death Valley, Albuquerque/Santa Fe, New York City, and Boston.

ANN RAIA is Professor Emerita of Classics at the College of New Rochelle, where she founded and directed the Honors Program from 1974 to 2001. A member of NCHC since 1974, she served several terms on the Executive Committee, the Small College Honors Programs Committee, the Portz Committee, and the Honors Semesters Committee. She directed the 1984 United Nations Honors Semester and the 1996 New York City Honors Semester.

MICHAELA RUPPERT SMITH teaches academic writing, English and world literature, and interdisciplinary courses at Glion Institute of Higher Education and LRG University of Applied Sciences in Switzerland. She is a former teacher at the International Baccalaureate Program at Collège du Léman in Geneva, Switzerland. She has been actively involved with NCHC since 2001, when she directed the Midwestern State University Honors Program. She earned her PhD in intellectual history from Claremont Graduate University and her BA from Bryn Mawr College.

REBEKAH STONE participated in United Nations III in 1984. She currently lives in Atlanta.

ABOUT THE NCHC MONOGRAPH SERIES

The Publications Board of the National Collegiate Honors Council typically publishes two to three monographs a year. The subject matter and style range widely: from handbooks on nuts-and-bolts practices and discussions of honors pedagogy to anthologies on diverse topics addressing honors education and issues relevant to higher education.

The Publications Board encourages people with expertise interested in writing such a monograph to submit a prospectus. Prospective authors or editors of an anthology should submit a proposal discussing the purpose or scope of the manuscript; a prospectus that includes a chapter by chapter summary; a brief writing sample, preferably a draft of the introduction or an early chapter; and a *curriculum vitae*. All monograph proposals will be reviewed by the NCHC Publications Board.

Direct all proposals, manuscripts, and inquiries about submitting a proposal to the General Editor of the Monograph Series:

Dr. Jeffrey A. Portnoy
General Editor, Monograph Series
Honors Program
Georgia Perimeter College
555 N. Indian Creek Drive
Clarkston, GA 30021-2396

jeffrey.portnoy@gpc.edu

(678) 891-3620

NCHC Monographs & Journals

Assessing and Evaluating Honors Programs and Honors Colleges: A Practical Handbook by Rosalie Otero and Robert Spurrier (2005, 98pp). This monograph includes an overview of assessment and evaluation practices and strategies. It explores the process for conducting self-studies and discusses the differences between using consultants and external reviewers. It provides a guide to conducting external reviews along with information about how to become an NCHC-Recommended Site Visitor. A dozen appendices provide examples of "best practices."

Beginning in Honors: A Handbook by Samuel Schuman (Fourth Edition, 2006, 80pp). Advice on starting a new honors program. Covers budgets, recruiting students and faculty, physical plant, administrative concerns, curriculum design, and descriptions of some model programs.

Fundrai$ing for Honor$: A Handbook by Larry R. Andrews (2009, 160pp). Offers information and advice on raising money for honors, beginning with easy first steps and progressing to more sophisticated and ambitious fundraising activities.

A Handbook for Honors Administrators by Ada Long (1995, 117pp). Everything an honors administrator needs to know, including a description of some models of honors administration.

A Handbook for Honors Programs at Two-Year Colleges by Theresa James (2006, 136pp). A useful handbook for two-year schools contemplating beginning or redesigning their honors program and for four-year schools doing likewise or wanting to increase awareness about two-year programs and articulation agreements. Contains extensive appendices about honors contracts and a comprehensive bibliography on honors education.

The Honors College Phenomenon edited by Peter C. Sederberg (2008, 172pp). This monograph examines the growth of honors colleges since 1990: historical and descriptive characterizations of the trend, alternative models that include determining whether becoming a college is appropriate, and stories of creation and recreation. Leaders whose institutions are contemplating or taking this step as well as those directing established colleges should find these essays valuable.

Honors Composition: Historical Perspectives and Contemporary Practices by Annmarie Guzy (2003, 182pp). Parallel historical developments in honors and composition studies; contemporary honors writing projects ranging from admission essays to theses as reported by over 300 NCHC members.

Honors Programs at Smaller Colleges by Samuel Schuman (Third Edition, 2011, 80pp). Practical and comprehensive advice on creating and managing honors programs with particular emphasis on colleges with fewer than 4,000 students.

If Honors Students Were People: Holistic Honors Higher Education by Samuel Schuman (2013, 256pp). What if Honors students were people? What if they were not disembodied intellects but whole persons with physical bodies and questing spirits. Of course . . . they are. This monograph examines the spiritual yearnings of college students and the relationship between exercise and learning.

Inspiring Exemplary Teaching and Learning: Perspectives on Teaching Academically Talented College Students edited by Larry Clark and John Zubizarreta (2008, 216pp). This rich collection of essays offers valuable insights into innovative teaching and significant learning in the context of academically challenging classrooms and programs. The volume provides theoretical, descriptive, and practical resources, including models of effective instructional practices, examples of successful courses designed for enhanced learning, and a list of online links to teaching and learning centers and educational databases worldwide.

The Other Culture: Science and Mathematics Education in Honors edited by Ellen B. Buckner and Keith Garbutt (2012, 296pp). A collection of essays about teaching science and math in an honors context: topics include science in society, strategies for science and non-science majors, the threat of pseudoscience, chemistry, interdisciplinary science, scientific literacy, philosophy of science, thesis development, calculus, and statistics.

NCHC Monographs & Journals

Partners in the Parks: Field Guide to an Experiential Program in the National Parks by Joan Digby with reflective essays on theory and practice by student and faculty participants and National Park Service personnel (2010, 272pp). This monograph explores an experiential-learning program that fosters immersion in and stewardship of the national parks. The topics include program designs, group dynamics, philosophical and political issues, photography, wilderness exploration, and assessment.

Place as Text: Approaches to Active Learning edited by Bernice Braid and Ada Long (Second Edition, 2010, 128pp). Updated theory, information, and advice on experiential pedagogies developed within NCHC during the past 35 years, including Honors Semesters and City as Text™, along with suggested adaptations to multiple educational contexts.

Preparing Tomorrow's Global Leaders: Honors International Education edited by Mary Kay Mulvaney and Kim Klein (2013, 400pp). A valuable resource for initiating or expanding honors study abroad programs, these essays examine theoretical issues, curricular and faculty development, assessment, funding, and security. The monograph also provides models of successful programs that incorporate high-impact educational practices, including City as Text™ pedagogy, service learning, and undergraduate research.

Setting the Table for Diversity edited by Lisa L. Coleman and Jonathan D. Kotinek (2010, 288pp). This collection of essays provides definitions of diversity in honors, explores the challenges and opportunities diversity brings to honors education, and depicts the transformative nature of diversity when coupled with equity and inclusion. These essays discuss African American, Latina/o, international, and first-generation students as well as students with disabilities. Other issues include experiential and service learning, the politics of diversity, and the psychological resistance to it. Appendices relating to NCHC member institutions contain diversity statements and a structural diversity survey.

Shatter the Glassy Stare: Implementing Experiential Learning in Higher Education edited by Peter A. Machonis (2008, 160pp). A companion piece to *Place as Text*, focusing on recent, innovative applications of City as Text™ teaching strategies. Chapters on campus as text, local neighborhoods, study abroad, science courses, writing exercises, and philosophical considerations, with practical materials for instituting this pedagogy.

Teaching and Learning in Honors edited by Cheryl L. Fuiks and Larry Clark (2000, 128pp). Presents a variety of perspectives on teaching and learning useful to anyone developing new or renovating established honors curricula.

Writing on Your Feet: Reflective Practices in City as Text™ edited by Ada Long (2014, 160pp). A sequel to the NCHC monographs *Place as Text: Approaches to Active Learning* and *Shatter the Glassy Stare: Implementing Experiential Learning in Higher Education*, this volume explores the role of reflective writing in the process of active learning while also paying homage to the City as Text™ approach to experiential education that has been pioneered by Bernice Braid and sponsored by NCHC during the past four decades.

Journal of the National Collegiate Honors Council (JNCHC) is a semi-annual periodical featuring scholarly articles on honors education. Articles may include analyses of trends in teaching methodology, articles on interdisciplinary efforts, discussions of problems common to honors programs, items on the national higher education agenda, and presentations of emergent issues relevant to honors education.

Honors in Practice (HIP) is an annual journal that accommodates the need and desire for articles about nuts-and-bolts practices by featuring practical and descriptive essays on topics such as successful honors courses, suggestions for out-of-class experiences, administrative issues, and other topics of interest to honors administrators, faculty, and students.

NCHC Publication Order Form

Purchases may be made by calling 402-472-9150, emailing nchc@unl.edu, visiting our website <http://www. nchchonors.org>, or mailing a check or money order payable to: NCHC • 1100 Neihardt Residence Center • University of Nebraska–Lincoln • 540 N. 16th Street • Lincoln, NE 68588-0627.   FEIN 52–1188042

	Member	Non-Member	No. of Copies	Amount This Item
Monographs:				
Assessing and Evaluating Honors Programs and Honors Colleges: A Practical Handbook*	$25.00	$45.00		
Beginning in Honors: A Handbook (4th Ed.)	$25.00	$45.00		
Fundrai$ing for Honor$: A Handbook*	$25.00	$45.00		
A Handbook for Honors Administrators	$25.00	$45.00		
A Handbook for Honors Programs at Two-Year Colleges*	$25.00	$45.00		
The Honors College Phenomenon	$25.00	$45.00		
Honors Composition: Historical Perspectives and Contemporary Practices	$25.00	$45.00		
Honors Programs at Smaller Colleges (3rd Ed.)*	$25.00	$45.00		
If Honors Students Were People: Holistic Honors Higher Education	$25.00	$45.00		
Inspiring Exemplary Teaching and Learning: Perspectives on Teaching Academically Talented College Students*	$25.00	$45.00		
The Other Culture: Science and Mathematics Education in Honors	$25.00	$45.00		
Partners in the Parks: Field Guide to an Experiential Program in the National Parks	$25.00	$45.00		
Place as Text: Approaches to Active Learning (2nd Ed.)	$25.00	$45.00		
Preparing Tomorrow's Global Leaders: Honors International Education	$25.00	$45.00		
Setting the Table for Diversity	$25.00	$45.00		
Shatter the Glassy Stare: Implementing Experiential Learning in Higher Education	$25.00	$45.00		
Teaching and Learning in Honors*	$25.00	$45.00		
Writing on Your Feet: Reflective Practices in City as Text™	$25.00	$45.00		
Journals:				
Journal of the National Collegiate Honors Council (JNCHC) Specify Vol/Issue ____/____	$25.00	$45.00		
Honors in Practice (HIP) Specify Vol ____	$25.00	$45.00		
Total Copies Ordered and Total Amount Paid:				$

Name_____ Institution _____

Address _____

City, State, Zip _____

Phone _____ Fax_____ Email _____

*Print-on-Demand publications—will be delivered in 4-6 weeks.

Shipping costs will be calculated on the number of items purchased.

Apply a 20% discount if 10+ copies are purchased.